LIVE IT!

Naomi

Be encouraged!

Shelley

LIVE IT!

A DAILY DEVOTIONAL FOR STUDENTS

■BECKY TIRABASSI

ZondervanPublishingHouse
Grand Rapids, Michigan

A Division of HarperCollins*Publishers*

Requests for information should be addressed to:
Zondervan Publishing House
Grand Rapids, Michigan 49530

Library of Congress Cataloging-in-Publication Data

Tirabassi, Becky, 1954–
  Live it! / Becky Tirabassi
    p. cm.
    Summary: Daily devotions discuss how to live in relationship with
God, other people, and yourself.
    ISBN 0-310-53751-7 (pbk.)
    1. Teenagers—United States—Prayer-books and devotions—
English. [1. Prayer books and devotions.] I. Title.
  BV4850.T57   1991
  248.8'3—dc20   91–10206
                                                                    CIP
                                                                     AC

Edited by Tim Stafford and Verne Becker
Designed by Rachel Hostetter
Illustrated by Robert McCoy
Cover design by the Aslan Group, Ltd.

Printed in the United States of America

94   95 / CH / 10   9   8   7   6   5   4   3

ABOUT THE YOUTHSOURCE™ PUBLISHING GROUP

YOUTHSOURCE™ books, tapes, videos, and other resources pool the expertise of three of the finest youth-ministry resource providers in the world:

> **Campus Life Books**—publishers of the award-winning *Campus Life* magazine, for nearly fifty years helping high schoolers live Christian lives.

> **Youth Specialties**—serving ministers to middle-school, junior-high, and high-school youth for over twenty years through books, magazines, and training events such as the National Youth Workers Convention.

> **Zondervan Publishing House**—one of the oldest, largest, and most respected evangelical Christian publishers in the world.

Campus Life
465 Gundersen Dr.
Carol Stream, IL 60188
708/260-6200

Youth Specialties
1224 Greenfield Dr.
El Cajon, CA 92021
619/440-2333

Zondervan
1415 Lake Dr., S.E.
Grand Rapids, MI 49506
616/698-6900

Dedicated to Amy Lavender

Thanks for all your help:
Amy,
Tim,
Tic,
Chic,
Rog, Jake, and Rick

CONTENTS

LIVING

in

Relationship

WITH

GOD

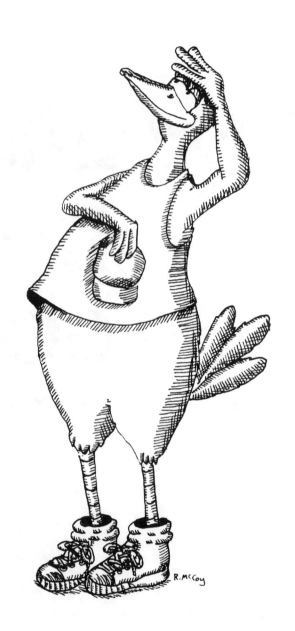

LIVE IT! *in faith*

Faith vs. Fear on the Slopes

Being a rookie skier, I was crazy to go up the mile-high lift in Brianhead, Utah. Somehow, though, my high schoolers talked me into it. They assured me it would be "rad" and that I'd cruise down just fine.

On the way up the chair lift, I turned back to look over my shoulder . . . and that's when I started to get real nervous. The fear that I had tried to shove down started creeping up my back and out my turtleneck! I was trembling by the time I tumbled off the lift. (Even getting off the lift on both skis was a feat for me!) And like a kitten stuck in a tree, afraid to come down, I froze, wishing I could turn back.

As youth director, I had told these very same kids to *have faith* and not to let fears overcome them. Now the roles had switched! They had to convince their "adult" leader that she really was going to make it down that mountain in one piece.

Perching on the edge of the slope, I couldn't believe how steep it looked. I kept trying to muster my courage, trying to convince myself that I wouldn't get hurt. The others were growing tired of waiting for me, and I finally had to admit there was only one "cool" option to get down—SKI!

I was nearly paralyzed by fear. Yet, having no other choice, I spiked one pole on each side of me into the snow and bent my knees. Then I began to have second thoughts, but it was too late—the forward momentum plunged my body toward the first dip and into the air!

From that point on, the kids coached me through each part of the run, picked me up when I wiped out, and helped me untangle my skis and poles and bindings. Their encouraging words gave me extra strength—*until* I looked down the next slope. How would I ever make it down? Then I would hear them holler, "C'mon, Becks—you can do it!"

The clincher came when everyone headed to the trails—except for me and Chadd, a freshman football player. I hated being left behind, yet I knew I couldn't hold up the group any longer. Chadd must have seen the pale look on my face; I guess he felt sorry for me. He didn't seem like the most outwardly spiritual teenager I'd ever met, so he thoroughly surprised me when he said, "Becks, do you wanna pray?"

Here I was, the fearless leader shaking in her ski boots, listening to a high school freshman gently reminding me to put my faith in God. We prayed a simple prayer, and I thought to myself, "I've gotta make it now, or . . ."

What a flight! What a blast! My fears had almost kept me from experiencing one of the greatest times of my life. I *did* make it to the bottom, and as the week progressed, I whooshed over trails and jumps and dips and powder. When I think about that trip, I can hardly wait to go back and do it all over!

When it comes to giving their whole lives to Christ, many people freeze. They are overwhelmed by fear. They imagine the worst: *What will I miss out on? What will I have to give up?*

Faith is letting go of your fears. It's taking flight. It's expecting not the worst, but the *best* of a new life in Christ! It's a challenge and an adventure—with jumps and trails and dips and powder. And because bruises and falls are inevitable at times, it's really important to have a group of "ski chums" to encourage you along the way—people who've been there before, who know your fears and can coach you through them, people who may even get you to try something new! And one day down the road you'll stop and ask yourself, "Why didn't I do this sooner? What was I waiting for?"

• • • • •
LIVE IT OUT!

Ask yourself, "Have I really given all of my life to Christ—in faith? Have I let go? Am I still holding on to something that is keeping me from experiencing a fuller life of faith in Christ?" Perhaps now is the time to hop on the lift and have the time of your life. Start now by reading Galatians 2:20 and Ephesians 2:8–9.

Faith Comes from Hearing

I watched her walk toward me from the youth building. Her face told me she was sad, maybe even ashamed. Her slow pace told me that what she wanted to talk about would not be easy.

"I'm losing my faith," she said in a shaky voice. She avoided my eyes, and I could sense her discouragement. "I'm starting to lose my strength and the beliefs that have kept me strong."

I appreciated her honesty, and gently encouraged her to continue. "When did you first notice this?"

"Oh, about a month ago . . ." Her voice trailed off, and I could see her thoughts wandering back to when she felt strong in the Lord.

"How's your quiet time?" I asked, trying to look into her eyes.

"Well, uh, I've kinda been too busy to read my Bible or pray," she stammered. "And then there's my job—well, you know how it goes."

A thought occurred to me. "How long do you think it's been since you've read your Bible regularly and had a daily time of prayer?"

"Oh, about a month or so."

I didn't want to sound like I was dishing out a magic formula; I truly wanted to encourage my friend. So we sat down and talked about the basics of being a Christian. I explained how one's faith is *fueled* by the Bible.

The result? Our conversation led to a little "pact" between us: She would work at establishing a regular time to focus on God and his Word, and I would check in on her periodically to see how she was doing. Just the relief of knowing that someone cared about her and was willing to help made her smile. Instead of scuffling away with her head down, she ran to meet the rest of the students!

I'm convinced that faith is fundamentally crucial to Christians, for it (1) determines their strength and courage, and (2) affects their choices and decisions. The Bible is simple and clear about the key to gaining more faith whenever we need it. The key? "Faith comes from hearing the message, and the message is heard through the word of Christ" (Romans 10:17).

When I feel my faith weakening, I open my Bible. I ask God to show me (1) a personal "word," (2) a promise, or (3) a special passage I can read to be encouraged by him personally. A basic concordance, cross-reference guide, commentary, or Bible dictionary can quickly alert me to Scriptures that will lift my spirits, deepen my faith, and strengthen my understanding of God's purposes for my life.

• • • • •
LIVE IT OUT!

Rate your faith today by considering the following questions:

How often do you read your Bible? _____

Would you like more faith? _____

Where will you begin reading today? (Begin in Romans if you need someplace to start.) _____

"Just Trust the Lord!"

When you can't see the end of the tunnel . . . when there are no answers to the overwhelming crisis you're in . . . when you don't understand anything that's happening to you . . . that's when your good ol' Christian friend (in all sincerity) tells you, "Just trust the Lord!" But what does it really mean, *in practice*, to "just trust the Lord?" Try this:

TAKE REFUGE,

RELY ON GOD'S WAYS,

UNDERSTAND HIS WORD,

STEP OUT and

TURN FROM THE WORLD.

TRUST is **Taking refuge in the Lord** (Psalm 91:1–2). Imagine yourself protected by his tower of refuge! He is there—your strength, your security, your shield against a powerful enemy or a terrible situation that threatens you.

TRUST is **Relying on his ways, not yours** (Isaiah 55:8–9). Read Isaiah 55 and remind yourself that "his ways are not our ways." Our solutions, our insights, our ideas may or may not resolve the problem, but God assures us that he has a way!

TRUST is **Understanding the Word** (2 Timothy 3:16–17). Every day God has a word for us. And anyone who reads, memorizes, meditates on, and knows how to apply the Word of God knows that his promises are available to all who put their trust in him.

TRUST is **Stepping out on a limb** (Proverbs 16:9). At this point in your life, are you walking *with* God or *without* him? Is there any area of your life that you need to go "out on a limb" and trust him to surround you? Walking with God now is a big part of trusting him with your future.

TRUST is **Turning from the world's ways** (Romans 12:2). It's tough in America today not to look, think, and act like the "world." Why? One reason is that the "world" surrounds us—it invades our school, our friends, music, TV, clothes. When we put our trust in God, however, we say to him, "Change my thinking—renew my mind—so that I begin to look, think, and act according to your will. And I'll trust you with the results." Go for it!

● ● ● ● ●
LIVE IT OUT!

First, take a little time in this blank space to talk to God about (1) a current situation in which you need to trust him more, or (2) a recent past experience in which you failed to trust him enough. Tell God your feelings, confess if you need to, and ask for his help:

_____

_____

_____

_____

_____

Then begin a list of verses under these headings that you can refer to later:

When I Need to . . .

Take Refuge:	Rely on God's Ways:	Understand His Word:	Step Out:	Turn from the World:
_____	_____	_____	_____	_____
_____	_____	_____	_____	_____
_____	_____	_____	_____	_____
_____	_____	_____	_____	_____

Lean on Me

Should I buy a red car or a white Jeep? Should I take chemistry now or next semester? Should I ask Mary to the dance . . . or Lynn? Should I take a summer job at the mall or be a volunteer camp counselor? Should I go on vacation with their family or mine?

When faced with a decision, large or small, how do you choose? The Bible says, "Trust in the Lord with all your heart and lean not on your own understanding; in all your ways acknowledge him, and he will make your paths straight" (Proverbs 3:5–6).

Some of us, having avoided God's way, have had to learn things the hard way. But God's guidance, help, and direction from the Word will save a lot of heartache, disappointment, and loss if it is followed!

Many of us carry incredible scars from when we avoided or ignored God's advice. And though it's not intentional, somehow our *desire* for something we want can overshadow our need to consult God, or even to follow what we know to be right. As ancient as it seems, the book of Proverbs is actually a practical, relevant guide to living the Christian life. Chapter after chapter is filled with simple but solid advice. See for yourself.

Should I "follow the crowd?"	Read Proverbs 1:10–19
Is morality out-dated?	Read Proverbs 2:16–19
How can I be wise?	Read Proverbs 3:1–8; 4:5–27
Affairs? Adultery?	Read Proverbs 5:15–23; 6:23; 7
What's better than money?	Read Proverbs 8:10–11
What's wrong with a little fool-ishness?	Read Proverbs 9:13–18; 10:1
What's the point of being a prude?	Read Proverbs 11:20 and 12:23
A quick temper?	Read Proverbs 13:1; 14:3; 15:1–2
Plans? Decisions?	Read Proverbs 16:1–3, 7, 9
Pride—and the tongue	Read Proverbs 17:7, 28; 18:2; 19:19, 27

The price of procrastination	Read Proverbs 20:4; 21:5; 22:26–27
Taking advice	Read Proverbs 23:22–23; 24:6
Honor and integrity	Read Proverbs 25:6–7; 26:28; 27:1–2
Accepting criticism	Read Proverbs 28:13–14; 29:1
Advice for life	Read Proverbs 30:32
The signs of an exceptional woman	Read Proverbs 31:10–31

• • • • •

LIVE IT OUT!

A proverb a day has a powerful way of having an effect on your day! Choose a topic and at least one Proverb from the above list that interests you. Read the passages and then write about how that verse can/should/will affect your life—now and in the future:

Topic	Proverb	How does it apply to me now?	How can it apply to me in the future?

Other sources for getting more out of the book of Proverbs are *The Narrated Bible* and *The Student Bible* (Zondervan).

"I Just Wanna Die ..."

One morning after a long drinking binge, I woke up in a strange apartment, with no idea of how I got there or what I had done along the way. I felt completely ashamed of myself, disgusted in who I had become, and nauseated with self-hate. I couldn't face my parents, because they were part of the problem. I couldn't tell my friends because I worried that they would reject me. And I couldn't tell my boss because I was afraid she would fire me. I felt certain that if they knew the truth about me, they would never love or accept me again.

At that point in my life, I thought there was only one way to stop the pain: suicide. Thankfully, I never got far enough to plan the "how" of killing myself, but I was feeling overwhelmed by desperation and hopelessness.

Thinking about suicide is a scary thing. I know. I also know of *many* students who've considered it and even tried it. And because I freely share my past when I speak, I seem to relate to students who have felt many of the same things I once did.

One junior in high school—a cute, funny, outgoing girl—recently attempted suicide with an overdose of pills. Her mother encouraged her to talk with me about her problems. Neither of us likes to sit in an office, so we took off together for a long drive.

Before long she had given me three reasons why her life wasn't worth living anymore:

Loneliness—an unexpected breakup with her boyfriend.

Family feuds—high expectations from her parents and competition between siblings for their parents' approval.

Poor grades—classes required more effort than she had given or expected, resulting in low marks and low self-esteem.

Knowing that many students have felt these same thoughts—maybe even you who are reading this—I want to remind you that:

You are not alone. Many students face the very same disappointments you do—divorced parents, alcoholism, drug addiction, broken relationships, abuse, shattered dreams, and frustrated expectations. But there are people, places, churches, organizations, groups, and counselors who are trained specifically to help you right now.

Don't let another day go by—take the step or pick up the phone and ask someone to help you.

God promises that he is with you. He is, you know, he really is. When Joshua faced an overwhelming assignment, God told him, "Be strong and courageous. Do not be terrified; do not be discouraged, for the Lord your God will be with you wherever you go" (Joshua 1:9). And he assured Joshua that he would never leave him or forsake him (1:5). Neither will he let go of you. "Hold unswervingly" to this hope, Hebrews 10:23 encourages us, "for he who promised *is* faithful." When there is no human hope left, God *is* there to hold on to you. Grab on to him with all of your might. Put your hope in his name and his Word. He will *never* leave you. Ask him to come alongside of you, to bring you help, relief, and comfort. I know he will be there, because he says he will. Let his Word bring hope into your day.

• • • • •

LIVE IT OUT!

I want to *strongly* urge you to:

Get help. Sometimes people around you do not understand all that you are feeling. *You* need to tell someone if you have had thoughts of suicide.

Don't be afraid of what friends might think. There will *always* be certain people who might disapprove of you, drop you, or reject you when you are struggling. Sadly, that's a fact of life. So if you need help, don't wait until you think others around you will understand. True friends will always be there for you—they may not agree or partake, but they won't ridicule or reject you.

Remember that God is faithful. Hold on.
Hold unswervingly to your hope in God—for he is faithful!
Read Hebrews 10:23, 36 and Romans 8:28–39.

Touching Your Dreams

Just as a gardener puts seeds into soil, God puts dreams into our hearts and minds—with the expectation that they will grow into something great.

A thought or an idea from God takes hold in your heart and doesn't seem to leave. It may be months or years before you realize your dream—or even touch it. But if it is from God, he will open the doors in his timing and allow your plans to succeed (Proverbs 16:3). Remember, if it is *his* idea, he wants it for *you*, too!

From the very beginning of my conversion to Christ, I believed I should write a book for students about how lost I was as an alcoholic and the dramatic turnaround that occurred when I met Christ. It was *seven years* after I became a Christian that a publisher talked to me about the project, *another two years* before the book was written, and *yet another year* before it was published. Sure, it was a long wait for a dream to come true. But every time I look at the cover of *Life of the Party*, or talk to someone who's been helped by it, I touch that dream!

Four years ago, I again felt strongly that God was encouraging me to write—this time a daily devotional for students. *I* wanted to do it, and I told my friends I thought *God* wanted me to do it, but nothing happened initially with the idea. I decided to pray about it every day.

More than two years later, I got a phone call from someone I had only met twice. "Would you be willing to write a devotional for every student to receive at our youth convention?" he asked me.

Though I was amazed at precisely how the book materialized, I wasn't surprised to receive the call, because I had been *expecting* God to answer my prayer—someday! And since I had never told this person I had been praying for two years about a devotional, I felt convinced that now was the time to touch my dream—God's dream. (As you read this, you're touching my dream, too!)

• • • • •
LIVE IT OUT!

What dream has God given you? What thought or idea just won't go away? _____

_____

_____

What things do you really like to do—sing, write, fly, speak, sew, or build? _____

_____

In what direction might God be leading you—medicine, missions, athletics, music, teaching? _____

_____

Has God been using your parents, pastor, or Christian counselors to nudge you in a certain direction? _____

_____

List one or two dreams you believe God has given you as *lifetime* goals. Then write out the words of Psalm 37:4–5 and memorize them this week.

_____

_____

Faith Is...

".... being sure of what we hope for and certain of what we do not see." That's faith, according to Hebrews 11:1. But how can we hope in what we cannot see?

Imagine being Noah. God asks you to build a huge covered barge in your front yard! Do you go ahead and do it? How many jokes will you be the butt of? How stupid will you feel?

Or how about Abraham? Ninety-something years old, no children, and God tells him he'll be the father not only of a son, not even of a large family, but of a nation!

Do you want to have an incredible relationship with God? Then faith is essential.

• • • • •
LIVE IT OUT!

Hebrews 11:6 says, "Without faith it is impossible to please God, because anyone who comes to him must believe that he exists and that he rewards those who earnestly seek him."

What's your definition of faith? _____

_____

_____

When is it hard for you to have faith? _____

_____

_____

Think of a person who has faith that might serve as a role model for you. _____

_____

_____

In what area of your life do you need to have more faith? _____

_____

_____

_____

_____

_____

Read Hebrews 11 today.

LIVE IT! with Hope

Hope for Someone Special

Amy, a high-school junior who loves dancing and gymnastics, always seems to be assigned to my room at camp. We have a lot in common, but mostly we love to talk! This summer we ended up as roommates again, but something had changed.

Instead of bursting into camp, full of her usual enthusiasm, Amy almost didn't come. Why? As the week progressed, she told me she was at a spiritual low, caused by everything from guys to job to boredom. So we decided to get her back on track with the Lord by spending a day together at my house on the following Sunday.

Since I was working on this book at the time, I asked her if I could read some of the stories to get her opinion. Well, one day turned into four—and not only did Amy help me write *Live It!* from a student's perspective, but after so many hours of talking about God, she realized just how far she had slipped away from him.

On our third night, her boyfriend asked her over to his house. So I gave her a break and told her if she called me at a decent hour, I'd pick her up.

When she got in my car later that night, she gasped, "You won't believe what happened! Mike lives with his grandma, and while we were sitting inside, we heard a loud thump out on the porch. His grandma had fallen down and was groaning in pain. Mike ran outside, helped her into the house and put her on the couch. I was so afraid we'd have to take her to the hospital!

"As I looked at his grandma hurting on the couch, I thought, *I've got to pray for her.* So I began to pray silently, but immediately another thought crossed my mind: *I haven't even thought about praying in situations like this for a long time. Wow—maybe I'm getting back on track!'*

Amy had rediscovered a wonderful truth: that praying to God revives a hope within us—a hope that believes in his ability to deliver, to rescue, and to bring healing! Like rekindling an old friendship, talking to God again can bring back great memories, which in turn give us hope.

And, by the way, Grandma *didn't* have to go to the hospital!

● ● ● ● ●

LIVE IT OUT!

When is the last time you looked to God as your *immediate* source of hope rather than your last resort? Be encouraged to put your hope in God for *every* detail of your life.

Read 1 Peter 5:6–7, and then write it out in your own words:

_____

_____

_____

_____

_____

_____

_____

_____

_____

Hope...When You're Hurting

"Lord,

Here I am, not sure of what I'm doing here or who I am.

After being pulled under several times this week, my self-image can barely stay afloat. If another wave hits, I may go under.

Does anybody really understand? Does anybody care how I feel—how much I'm hurting?

I guess that's why I turn to you, God.

You love me.
> You know me.
>> You plan for me.
>> You listen to me.

And you, Creator of all, created me."

One of my greatest sources of hope is in reading and praying the Psalms. Many of the Psalms are King David's own prayers to God for help, forgiveness, and direction. By reading and then rephrasing the verses in my own words—my own feelings—I gain new hope, confidence, and direction for my own life.

• • • • •

LIVE IT OUT!

Make Psalm 139 your prayer today. Slowly read it out loud as a prayer, or choose specific verses and rewrite them using your own words. To give you an idea of how to do this, here is my version of verses 1–5:

O Lord, you know *all* about me.

You know every time I sit or stand.

You know my every thought!

You know *why* I do the things I do. . . . You are familiar with all my ways.

Even before I talk to someone, you know everything I will say!

You go before me and behind me. Your hand is on me! There is *nowhere* I can go and not be with you.

I'm so glad you know me and *still* love me!

Try it yourself:

_____

_____

_____

_____

_____

Hope ... When You Feel Like Giving Up

Jake, my eleven-year-old son, lay on the living room rug with his schoolbook. "Mom," he whined in despair, "I'll *never* get my new Nintendo game."

A ten-day vacation during the school year had set him back. Now he faced reading twenty-six more chapters of his book in order to get caught up before the end of the term. If he completed it all on time, he would earn his reward—a Nintendo game. To Jake, the impossible loomed ahead. But from my perspective, I could quickly tabulate the hours and days left and how long it would take for him to finish. I knew he *could* do it, if only he wouldn't give up!

"Jake," I said, "just read two chapters now before dinner and then we'll read a bunch together after dinner."

He looked over his shoulder at me, wanting to believe me, yet still paralyzed by the overwhelming task ahead.

I had to prod, beg, encourage, and convince him that it *could* be done. At last—and I mean at *last*, he agreed to give it a try. After reading seven chapters, he actually could smile again. He thought again about his new Nintendo game. It would be hard work, but if he tackled his reading chapter by chapter, he'd be able to reach his goal.

All people go through periods of discouragement as they strive to reach a goal, yet feel overwhelmed with the responsibility.

How can you get through those times?

First, *look to God*. Philippians 4:13 says, "I can do *everything* through him [Christ] who gives me strength." Ask *him* for help, ideas, strength, and renewed hope. How? Any way you like—out loud, silently, or in writing—that honestly expresses your feelings.

Second, *have a plan*.

Actually write out the steps you need to take to reach your goal. Then, *start doing them* —one at a time (Proverbs 14:23; 13:4).

Finally, *don't give up*. Don't let procrastination, intimidation, or desperation cause you to give up the plans God has set aside for you!

> "I know the plans I have for you," declares the Lord, "plans to prosper you and not to harm you, plans to give you hope and a future" (Jeremiah 29:11). Don't give up.

• • • • •

LIVE IT OUT!

Begin a conversation with God about a goal or dream (big or little) that you are about to give up on. Ask for his advice. Should you pursue it? If so, how?

List five steps you can take to reach your goal. Then, rather than give up on it, *go for it*, one step at a time:

TASK: _____

Step 1: _____

Step 2: _____

Step 3: _____

Step 4: _____

Step 5: _____

Now think of someone who can (1) help you complete this task and (2) keep you accountable so you can follow through to the end:

_____

Give them a call.

Hope ... When You're Disappointed, Rejected, Lonely, or Betrayed

You imagine the worst. And then the worst happens!
"No, they didn't call back."
"I'm sorry you didn't make it."
"She doesn't like you."
"No more spots available—try again next year."
"I'm sorry." Click.

"I'm sorry." Slam.

"I'm sorry." Silence.

I'll call him Chip. He found me by a tree after the general session at camp. He was nice looking and friendly, with a warm, genuine smile. As we chatted, he seemed a bit slow, but he had a wonderful attitude toward life, and toward God. His faith was simple and childlike, but very real. Then the conversation shifted from small talk to what he really was looking for—hope.

"Becky, what should I do?" he began, fighting back tears. His vulnerability caught me off guard. "I wanted to ask out a girl in my youth group. And I just found out . . ." he hesitated, trying to be strong, "that she doesn't like me. She doesn't like me at *all*!" Then a stuttered breathing moved from his chest up into his throat.

As I listened, my mind wandered through a maze of feelings and memories. My first thought was, "Where is that girl? I'm gonna kill her!" I've felt the stinging pain of rejection many times in my life. And sadly, I've done more than my share of giving others the shaft without realizing how much I was hurting them. But right now, I wanted to offer Chip hope in his own disappointment and pain.

"First of all," I said, "She obviously doesn't know what a nice person you are!" He smiled. "And you know, Chip, there will always be people like her around who don't take time to see the real you. In the years to come, you'll probably experience many lost loves and unreturned sentiments. Love is just like that.

"But we still get hurt sometimes. There's a little phrase that encourages me when I've been let down or rejected: 'God's delays are not God's denials.' It reminds me that God sees far ahead of me. What I think is perfect for now may not be his best for me. And ultimately, I truly want *his* best! I do. Even when it hurts.

"Chip, I can't begin to tell you how many times I've faced rejection, disappointment, and betrayal. Sometimes I cry, other times I fight back, but eventually I turn to God for help. Let's take a minute and talk to him, okay?"

Together we poured out our hearts to God in prayer. There were no *immediate* answers, but I think Chip felt a genuine sense of hope that God was there for him—and would continue to be there—at *all* times and in *all* circumstances!

As I read in the Bible about people such as Moses, Noah, and

Joseph, I see that in spite of their disappointment or rejection or doubt in what God was doing, they knew deep down they could place their future in his hands. Trusting in God gave them *hope* — to wait, to hold on, to hang in there, and to know that God will never leave, forsake, or abandon the children he loves. He will deliver!

• • • • •

LIVE IT OUT!

Read Psalm 40, verse by verse. Imagine yourself discussing with God your most current disappointment or rejection. Take hope in his timeless words. Trust him to help and deliver you. Copy the *one* verse below that really gives you hope.

_____

_____

_____

Hope ... When You're Homeless

At age seventeen I left home, eventually moved to California, and began living a lifestyle I'd be embarrassed now to detail. But at age twenty-one, I made a decision for Christ and experienced an incredible transformation—inside and out!

After about two months of hanging out with Christians, going to church, and reading my Bible, I called Ohio to ask my parents if I could come home—to tell them, and to *show* them, that I had changed.

As I waited for someone to answer the phone, a flood of

memories swept over me. I felt anxious, unsure of what they'd say or how they'd respond to me. We had known years of screaming, swearing, even physical fights when I had lived at home during my years of drug and alcohol addiction. Now I was afraid they might hang up on me or reject me. We had tried so many times to live together as a "happy" family—all without success. Each ring made me more nervous.

Finally my dad answered the phone—unusual in our house. And instead of asking for Mom, as I usually did, I simply said, "Dad, can I come home?"

I was certain he'd respond by reciting a bunch of rules and expectations, and then rehash the pitfalls of our past. But instead he said, "When should we expect you?"

I was stunned. Was he actually willing to wipe away the past and welcome me back, just like that?

Within three weeks, I had moved back home.

Some of you reading this book today may have drifted away from the Lord. It may seem impossible for you to come back "home," to be loved again, to be forgiven. But the Scriptures make it clear that God the Father waits for you to turn from where you've been, come back into his home and family, confess your sins and receive his forgiveness (1 John 1:9).

Turn from the ways
That have kept you from him.
Admit that you've sinned
And ask him to come in.

• • • • •

LIVE IT OUT!

If you've been away long, read Luke 15 and be assured that God does love you—no matter where you've been—and wants to welcome you home with open arms.

Come home today, won't you?

Hope ... When You've Failed

In 1974, history recorded the resignation of the President of the United States, Richard Nixon. One of his right-hand men was Chuck Colson, a tough and powerful attorney. Colson had risen to prominence by winning a Supreme Court case—the dream of every lawyer—before being named special counsel to the President. But because of his criminal involvement in the Watergate scandal, he was convicted and sent to prison.

In his book *Loving God*, Chuck writes that his greatest failure became God's greatest success in his life. He seemed to have lost everything—prestige, power, fame. But his humiliation and failure caused him to turn to Christ, whom he had ignored for years. As he sat in jail, he felt Christ's forgiveness beginning to wash away his guilt and give him a hope that his life could still be worth something.

As a "new man" in Christ, Chuck believed he was given a new purpose in life. He founded a ministry called Prison Fellowship that reaches out to thousands of prison inmates, sharing the power of the gospel and the forgiveness of Jesus Christ.

Perhaps you, like Chuck, have experienced failure. Often failure can cause us to think that the end is near—or even worse, has already arrived! Or that life simply can't go on, that things will never be the same.

At age twenty-one, I myself was an alcoholic and had experienced a major failure in my life. Disgusted at the person I had become and trapped by my addiction, I felt like I had no way out. Fortunately, in a dramatic turn of events, the janitor of a church led me to Jesus Christ. Looking back, I realize the most radical part of my story was being offered a new life—a new identity—in Christ. All I had to do was trade in my old one!

And like Chuck Colson, my greatest failure also motivated me to share the good news of Christ, which I've been doing for the last fourteen years of my life.

Romans 8:28 reminds us that "in all things God works for the good of those who love him, who have been called according to his purpose." God will take our failures—big or small—and turn them around. There *is* hope, even when we fail . . . even when we fail *big*.

• • • • •
LIVE IT OUT!

Maybe you have felt like a failure lately. It could be over *one* area that is slipping out of control, or maybe *everything* seems to be falling apart! In the space below, write out a brief prayer to God and ask him for a new start.

Lord, _____

_____

_____

_____

The Lord will meet you at your point of need. He will lift you up. Count on him. After you pray, read 2 Corinthians 5:17.

Hope ...
When You're
Stressed Out

Is stress just an adult problem? Does stress only come in the form of ulcers and heart problems and chain smoking?

I don't think so. For students, stress sometimes appears along with . . .

- extra weight
- inability to cope with parents' divorce
- acne
- broken relationships
- rejection
- loneliness
- even attempted suicide.

Being a student means living in a world *full* of pressure! But what can you do about it?

God has a way out. In Philippians 4:6, Paul says, "Don't worry about anything; instead, pray about everything." I take the Bible seriously, and when God says pray about *everything*, that's what I do! I figure that if he had exceptions, he would have listed them!

Jesus talked about worry (or stress) in Matthew 6:25–34. He said something like this: "Here's the deal, you guys—don't worry about your life, what you're going to eat or drink, or about your body (whether you are skinny, fat, short, or long), or what you're going to wear. Those who don't know me run after all those things, but your heavenly Father knows that you need them."

The last few verses give this advice: "But seek first his kingdom and his righteousness, and *all these things will be given to you* as well! Therefore do not worry about tomorrow, for tomorrow will worry about itself. Each day has enough trouble of its own." (Ain't that the truth!)

As I was writing this, a song about prayer and hope crossed my mind, but I couldn't remember the chorus to save my life. As I racked my brain, a thought occurred to me: *Well, why not ask God to help me remember it?* So I prayed. Within five minutes the song played over the radio!

> Isn't it amazing
> What a prayer can do

When it all seems hopeless,
It'll pull you through.[1]

• • • • •
LIVE IT OUT!

(1) Right now, name something in your life that you're stressed out about.

(2) Talk to God about it *now*; don't wait.

(3) This week, *every time* you find yourself worrying about it, stop and say a little prayer, asking God to help you with the situation and give you the ability to cope.

(4) Remember, he already knows what you need. *Don't worry about it*—pray about it.

LIVE IT! *in the Word*

Health on a Shelf

As a kid, I went to church every Sunday. My whole family did. It was the all-American thing to do! We were religious, I guess you could say, but not really Christians.

In my denomination, if you went to confirmation classes for two years, you were "confirmed" in front of the whole church in a white robe and you received a white Bible. And if you were real fortunate, you had a confirmation party afterwards and got money from your relatives.

Right about the time of my confirmation, I started to hate going to church. I never got to sleep in on any other day, and most of my close friends at school didn't have to go, so why did I?

When I moved away from home, I quit going to church altogether. Funny thing, though: In every apartment, dorm, or house that I lived in for the next five years, my white Bible rested on a shelf—never opened, but always there. Little did I realize that my spiritual and emotional health was shoved away with it!

By the time I turned twenty-one, my broken life was aching for healing and health. I had become an alcoholic and a speed addict, with nowhere to turn. But then I met this guy—a strange fellow, I thought—who would talk to me about Jesus.

"Hey, I know all about Jesus," I remember saying.

"You may know *about* him," he answered, "but do you *know* him?"

One day he asked me, "Do you have a Bible?" Sure I did—a white one . . . somewhere. He challenged me to open it, to read it. I thought he was nuts. Yet on one very desperate day in my life, I opened that book, frantically searching for something that made sense. And to my surprise, I never put it down. After years of sitting silently on a shelf, the little white Bible showed me a whole, new, healthy life in the days and months that followed. I'll always be indebted to the strange guy who challenged me to dust off my Bible and read it.

Where's your Bible now? On a shelf? Under your bed? In the car? Lost in the closet? Or is it close at hand? Find a good, visible place for your Bible. Keep it in sight. Pull it out. Read it today, and *every* day.

• • • • •
LIVE IT OUT!

If you would like to start (or restart) reading your Bible every day for at least five minutes, write out a simple prayer of commitment to God:

_____

_____

_____

_____

_____

_____

If you don't know where to start, try 2 Corinthians 5 or Philippians 4.

Open It, Hope in It

Imagine walking into your house after a long day at school, only to find a letter on the kitchen table addressed to you from . . .

> Bon Jovi?
> Janet Jackson?
> The President?
> Jesse Jackson?
> Billy Joel?
> Michael Jordan?
> Someone you really love?

Immediately you drop everything and rip it open! First, you look for special sentiments in the opening. Next, you quickly skim to the closing remarks, hoping for a meaningful ending. And then you slowly go back through every word of the letter, taking in all the comments, secrets, and promises this special person wanted to share with you.

God himself has sent letters to us in the form of his Word, the Bible, in order to "hit the spot," to meet us where we're at, and to give us hope when we can't seem to go on. When I approach the Bible with the same anticipation I'd have for a letter from the President, I gain a new appreciation for God's presence in my life.

Perhaps you've been looking everywhere for a ray of hope, a sign of God's love toward you or a bit of encouragement. Open his letter tonight, before the lights are out, and let him remind you that he loves you.

LIVE IT OUT!

I'm going to challenge you to try something. Think of an area in your life right now that you would like God to speak to you about, and write it here. _____

_____

Ask God, in prayer, for a Scripture verse to encourage you, give you hope or direction or perseverance while you wait on his will.

Then, over the next few days, read your Bible—your planned daily passages, as well as spontaneous portions. Write down the verses you believe God has given you to provide hope in your particular situation:

_____

_____

"My soul faints with longing for your salvation, but I have put my hope in your word. . . . Sustain me according to your promise, and I will live; do not let my hopes be dashed" (Psalm 119:81, 116).

From the Map of . . . God!

Driving around Southern California is incredibly difficult—unless you know *exactly* where you're going. When I first moved here, I spent more hours on the wrong freeway than on the right one. Why? I didn't have a good map.

Then I bought a Thomas Guide—a 200-page map of my area that included indexes, references, and close-up views of certain areas. It always got me exactly where I needed to go—as long as I took the time to get it out and read it!

The same thing happens when you don't know where to look for something in the Bible. Where do you start? What if you're wondering what God says about topics such as divorce, failure, cheating, relationships, or parents?

Since I tend to ask lots of questions, I've discovered two great resources right in my own Bible: the concordance and the cross-references. (Most "study Bibles" contain both of these tools; if your Bible does not, consider buying a study Bible such as the *NIV Study Bible*. Or you can purchase a concordance separately.) These resources are not intended to be confusing, or just for intellectuals—they are designed to help!

A *concordance* is a verse or passage-finder located in the back of your Bible. When you want to know where a verse is, but you can only remember some of the words in it, you identify a main word and look up that word in your concordance. Or, when you are curious about a certain topic, just search for the word of interest (love, peace, faith, etc.). Under each word appears a list of verses, beginning with the Old Testament and ending with the New. The words are listed in dictionary form so you can locate them easily. A concordance can be a helpful tool to increase your knowledge of a subject or to find the exact location of a verse.

A *cross-reference system* usually appears along with the text you're reading—either at the bottom, side, or middle of the page. Often little letters or numbers are placed above a word or at the end of a verse (similar to footnotes). When you match the code letter or number with its listing among the references, you'll be given the "address" of another verse or verses that have a similar meaning, or may be an exact quote of the verse you have just read. A word or theme search can be very interesting—even exciting—once you get started.

• • • • •
LIVE IT OUT!

Think of a verse you like, but don't know exactly where it's located. Then use a concordance to look up a key word within the verse. Is your verse listed? If not, you may need to choose another key word from the verse and check under that word.

The verse is: _____

Or try this. Look up the word *love* in a concordance. On a separate sheet of paper, list the verses given. Look up each one, and create your own commentary and Bible study on the topic. Share it with a friend.

Now, using a Bible with a cross-reference system, look up Romans 8:28. Go to the place on the same page where additional verses are listed that refer to verse 28. Look up each one. How does it support Romans 8:28? Does it give new meaning to the verse for you? _____

_____

_____

_____

Are there other words or verses you've been looking to understand better? Begin a list and search. It's amazing how much help a good map can provide!

Curling Up with the Good Book

Have you ever read a book that you couldn't put down? A book so full of intrigue, excitement, or suspense that it kept you up way past midnight?

One winter vacation, I went to Florida with another family. Each day I sat out by the pool with my high-school friend. I had brought along a huge novel—*Julie*, by Catherine Marshall—to entertain me through the long, hot days.

Within a few hours, I realized I didn't want to put the book down. It was *so* good, I didn't want to be interrupted for dinner. In fact, when I got to the mildly romantic part, I even read some of it out loud to my friend. But then she asked me to keep reading—it had captured her, too!

We must have been a sight: two adults, reading one book—out loud—at a public pool! But we didn't care. We thoroughly enjoyed *Julie*, finishing it off in only twenty-four hours!

Curling up with a good book is like getting outside of your own life and into the drama of someone else's, where you are offered an escape, a dream, or an adventure.

Jesus was a great storyteller. Wherever he spoke, crowds immediately gathered. He was so intriguing that people wouldn't even leave to eat—though they had been listening to him for hours. He had a way about him—humorous, gentle, direct, vivid, motivating, and life-changing. He communicated so well that people came from everywhere and dropped everything to hear him talk. Would you?

If Jesus showed up at your house tonight and just wanted to chat, would you be interested? Would you take time out from TV, phone calls, or eating to hear what he had to say? What would you ask him?

John, one of Jesus' disciples, described Jesus in an unusual way. He wrote: "In the beginning was the Word, and the Word was with God, and the Word was God. . . . The Word became flesh and made his dwelling among us" (John 1:1, 14). The greatest storyteller, Jesus, was God in the flesh. His Word, the Bible, is meant to be as intriguing to a believer today as it was when he walked on earth!

• • • • •
LIVE IT OUT!

The next time you curl up with *the* Good Book, picture Jesus standing before you, telling you the story, using his hands to illustrate, his voice to motivate, and his presence to captivate you.

He *is* the Word. Try out this approach on John 14, then on other passages that interest you.

Fog Free

All of my California buddies wear "rad" sunglasses of every imaginable shape and color, with brand names such as Frogskins, Sunclouds, Oakley Blades, Vaurnet, Ray-Ban, and so on. They tell me no one should live in California and not wear sunglasses!

Why? Well, not only do they look cool, but they also have a useful purpose: to filter out the sun's rays and make it easier to see while driving, biking, skiing, or sunning. Some glasses even have special coatings so they won't fog up in cold temperatures!

Fog free! Wouldn't it be great if our lives could be that way? That we could always know where we needed to go and exactly how to get there? That we would never stumble or trip or fall or get lost in a fog?

My California friends are convinced there is no other way to clear vision than special specs. In a way, I'm like my friends. When it comes to my life, I'm convinced that I can't go without the one thing that will make my vision clear!

That one thing is the Bible. Reading it is one of the best ways to know God's will. It filters out distractions and helps me focus on the real issues. It warns me so that I don't get tripped up or lost in a fog of confusion.

Because I feel so strongly about its value, I made a decision over ten years ago to read my Bible every day for the rest of my life. It's not really an optional activity for me—something I do if I have the time. It's a necessity.

I know myself too well. I'm always getting into situations where I need clear direction. Sometimes I have too many choices to make, or I feel unsure of which way is God's best for me.

In order to avoid making wrong or impulsive decisions, I look to the Word of God for advice. Not everything is black and white in the Bible. Not every issue is clearly defined. But I am convinced that if I want to know God's will for my life, I must search the Bible to understand his nature and his guidelines for living.

Please don't think I've always felt that Bible reading was so special, or that I've achieved perfect discipline in my life. At one time, I didn't care *at all* about God or his best for me. I made my own plans and based my decisions on my desires. Unfortunately, those days ended up in heartache, humiliation, and broken relationships. It still stings sometimes to think about those days.

Even today, I don't always feel like reading the Bible. But now that I know what it's like to live *with* God's Word as my guide, I'll never go back to living without it. It's too painful. It's too foggy.

● ● ● ● ●
LIVE IT OUT!

Perhaps today you might want to stop and pray about your life: "Dear God, what is your will for me? Where do you want me to go? What do you want me to be? Who am I to care for? And how am I to act?"

Have you consulted the Word lately regarding *God's* will for your life? Take some time now and ask him to clear up any lingering fog.

Read Psalms 119:9, 11, 133, 165; 37:31; and 19:11.

What's in It for Me?

Before we feel ready to commit ourselves to *anything*, a subtle but real thought goes through our minds: *What's in it for me? Why should I bother? Is it gonna be worth it?*

Perhaps you've asked yourself the same question about the Bible: *Why should I read it? What's in it for me?*

Interestingly, a great place to find real benefits to reading the Bible is the Bible itself—in particular, Psalm 119, David's own reflection on the value of God's Word. Take a few minutes now to read these verses, then underline or highlight some of the words listed below that have a special meaning to you right now.

The Word of God . . .

Keeps me pure	v. 9
Keeps me from sin	v. 11
Is my counselor	v. 24
Gives me strength	v. 28
Shows me my freedoms	v. 45
Comforts me when I hurt	v. 50
Promises me God's love	v. 76
Can be trusted	v. 86
Helps me when I'm wronged	v. 87
Makes me wise	v. 98
Gives me clear direction	v. 105
Makes me happy inside	v. 111
Is a place to go for safety	v. 114
Gives me a promise to hope in	v. 116
Lifts me up when I'm depressed	v. 143
Is meant to last forever	v. 152
Is my defense	v. 154
Gives me peace	v. 165
Will deliver me from trouble	v. 170

• • • • •

LIVE IT OUT!

Which verses stand out the most to you? _____

_____

_____

_____

_____

_____

Pick one verse from the list above to memorize this week. Write it out here and on an index card, and carry the card with you until you've got the verse firmly implanted in your memory.

_____

_____

If you're looking for New Testament Scriptures that refer to the Word of God, read Hebrews 4:12 and 2 Timothy 3:16–17.

If You Commit to It, Stick to It

Have you ever tried weight-lifting? The first few times it's kind of fun, but then the pain sets in and the repetition begins to get boring. How do you get through it? Add a few new machines. Increase the amount of weight you're using. Work out at different times of the day. Lift with a friend.

Why bother? Because without the regular discipline of lifting weights, you won't improve your strength, muscle tone, or fitness.

Bible reading is really not much different. Some days it just jams. Other days you dread the thought of it. But without the regular discipline of it, you won't experience the strength of character (spiritual "muscle tone") that comes with a regular workout.

Why does Bible reading get boring sometimes? The reasons could fill a page, and they'd vary for all of us. But the bottom-line truth still remains: Daily Bible reading produces supernatural results in a believer's life.

Remember Hebrews 12:11: "No discipline seems pleasant at the time, but painful. Later on, however, it produces a harvest of righteousness and peace for those who have been trained by it."

• • • •
LIVE IT OUT!

If you've never read through the Bible in a year, try *The One Year Bible* (Tyndale House), or some similarly organized book that provides Old and New Testament readings, a Psalm, and a Proverb for each day. In a notebook or in the back of your Bible, keep a running list of the verses that either convict you (challenge you to change) or comfort you. (Or just underline as you read them.) It is amazing how God uses what we read to speak directly to our hearts and situations (Hebrews 4:12) on any given day.

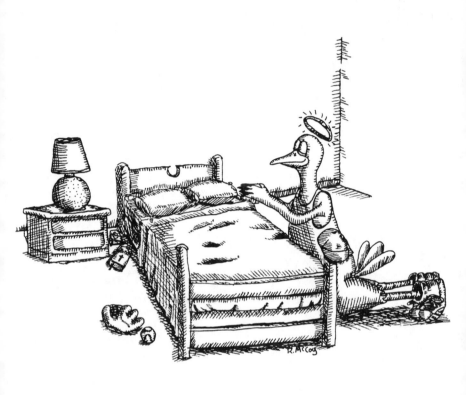

LIVE IT! and Pray

Attitude: Ask!

Six years ago I began a prayer list. Every day I pray for many people and plans and problems, and I'm always adding more to the list. The answers to these prayers have been phenomenal! Sometimes I receive an answer the same day, and other times I have to wait for years. Sometimes God completely closes the door and says no. But recording my requests each day, and *his* responses, has been a great faith adventure. It has really shown me that God does answer prayer!

Just what does God have to say about how we should pray? Does he say, "Don't ask," "Don't ask too often," or "Don't ask for little things?" See for yourself!

1. *Ask God about specific needs* (either in spoken, written, or silent prayer), then *look* for his answers! James writes, "You do not have, because you do not ask God" (4:2), and David says, "I lay my requests before you and wait in expectation" (Psalm 5:3). These scriptures encourage us to *ask* God, *expect* him to answer, *wait* for his answer, and *look* for his answer!

2. *Ask with a clean heart.* Read Mark 11:23–25, then ask yourself, "How's my heart?" Psalm 84:11 concurs: "No good thing does he withhold from those whose walk is blameless."

3. *Nothing is too little, simple, or crazy to talk to God about.*

Include him in *all* of your decisions and requests. Proverbs 3:5–6 says, "In *all* your ways acknowledge [or ask] him, and he *will* direct your paths."

4. *Persevere.* Hang in there and wait! As long as God hasn't said no, don't give up. In the early 1900s, George Mueller, a man of prayer, was said to have waited twenty-nine years before certain requests were answered! Study Luke 18:1–8, which was Jesus' reminder to "pray and not give up."

5. *Remember who you are asking.* Ephesians 3:20 reminds us that the one we are asking goes *beyond* all we can ask, imagine, or dream up!

6. *Remember that God hears you.* The psalmist writes, "Come and listen, all you who fear God; let me tell you what he has done for me. I cried out to him with my mouth; his praise was on my tongue. If I had cherished sin in my heart, the Lord would not have listened; but God has surely listened and heard my voice in prayer. Praise be to God, who has not rejected my prayer or withheld his love from me!" (66:16–20).

7. *Believe.* Mark 9:23 and 11:23–24 cause us to ask ourselves: Do I *expect* God to answer me? Do I *believe* he can or will answer my prayer? Do I believe he has the power to answer my prayer?

8. *Do something after you have prayed.* Take a step toward your request. "Ask and it will be given to you; seek and you will find; knock and the door will be opened to you" (Matthew 7:7).

9. *Expect the best.* Read Matthew 7:11. Would God give you anything less? Are you willing to wait for his best?

10. *Pray about everything!* Philippians 4:6–7 encourages us to pray about everything and not to worry about anything. If prayer dispels worry, which would you choose?

• • • • •
LIVE IT OUT!

Start a prayer request list and talk to God daily for at least one month. Then wait in expectation, recording God's answers as they occur. Oh, yes—one more thing: *ask,* but don't *tell* God how to answer your prayers!

Check It Out

It never fails. Someone says, "God doesn't answer my prayers, so why should I bother to pray?"

When I hear this, I want to ask: "Do you just talk to God when you are in trouble, or have you developed an ongoing relationship with him that includes talking with him *throughout* your day?"

Okay, since God really *wants* us to talk to him and make requests of him, he gives us a few guidelines in Scripture to check out our attitudes so we understand how prayer works. Take a few minutes to look up each of the following verses and briefly rephrase them:

James 4:3 _____

_____

_____

_____

Psalm 84:11b _____

_____

_____

_____

Psalm 37:4 _____

_____

_____

_____

1 Peter 3:12 _____

_____

_____

James 5:16 _____

_____

_____

From reading these verses it seems that "righteousness" is a quality God looks for in people who ask God to answer their prayers. Perhaps you can come up with a personal definition of a "blameless" or "righteous" life. Look up Psalms 15 and 24, then give it a try!

• • • • •
LIVE IT OUT!

Do you "walk your talk"? Ask yourself, "Am I making choices in my lifestyle and relationships that show others that I am a Christian?"_____

Is there a particular "sin" I might be holding on to, hiding, or enjoying? (See Galatians 5:19–21; Psalm 66:18.) _____

_____

If so, confess it as sin, so you can be a James 5:16 prayer—powerful and effective! _____

_____

Would You Agree?

On the day that I started my new life as a Christian, Ralph, the janitor who led me to Christ, asked me to *confess*—admit to

God—any sins I had committed that I could remember.

My eyes were closed when he asked me to do this, but a slew of images rushed into my mind—my drunken binges, my foul language, my lying, and definitely the immoral relationship with my boyfriend.

I realized I *wanted* to be free from the guilt of my sin. So I freely confessed all these things, and much more—out loud—to God. Poor Ralph! As he listened to my confessions, one by one, I'm sure his eyes must have grown as big as saucers. And after I admitted to God all those wrongdoings, I then asked him to forgive me and cleanse me!

Admitting a sin to God—or to anybody—is never easy. But agreeing with God by saying "I did this and it was wrong" removes our guilt and makes the way for a perfect God to supernaturally forgive.

On the other hand, sin *unconfessed* can make matters worse! When we cover up the truth, the guilt over the secret begins to separate us from those we love by increasing tension, grudges, and distance.

But God is not like people. He doesn't hold grudges. He doesn't scold or shake us. He says, "If we claim to be without sin, we deceive ourselves and the truth is not in us. If we confess our sins, he is faithful and just and will forgive us our sins and purify us from all unrighteousness" (1 John 1:8–9).

God's forgiveness actually *feels* good—and the relief from the guilt (that only *he* can grant) feels even better! A renewed relationship with God can begin any time we take that "admit" step with him.

• • • • •
LIVE IT OUT!

What's inside of you that has never been talked about with God? *He* knows about it, but maybe you just haven't *agreed* with him that it's a problem in your life. Would you share it with him today? Take as much time as you need to set the record straight.

Look Up,
Look Up!

One day I met a girl who had hit bottom. She'd done cocaine for so long that she couldn't stop—and she couldn't help herself. She was losing her family and her sanity.

Her mother had asked me to meet with her, and she practically dragged her eighteen-year-old daughter into my office. The girl's hard, cold look told me she was desperate.

She was desperate for . . .
love,
hope,
help,
and a fresh start.

She needed a way out of the pit of shame,
the pain of guilt,
the humiliation of failure and
the disappointment of self-hate.

I knew of only one way I could help her at that moment: *prayer.*

My favorite way to counsel people is to offer to pray with them. Often I begin by reading Psalm 62:8: "Trust in him at all times, O people; pour out your hearts to him, for God is our refuge."

"Would you like to pray?" I asked her.

"Yes," she replied, though she wouldn't pray her own prayer out loud. That was okay. I knew God would meet us. I believed God's power was available to her, as it had been to others in equally hopeless situations, and as it had been to me. I prayed for her, and then asked her to repeat these words:

"O God, touch my life with your powerful Holy Spirit. Change me, renew me, forgive me. I need you now—to feel your presence and your unconditional, unfailing love. Give me strength for today. Please give me hope for tomorrow."

She looked up and wiped away streams of tears. "Thanks," she whispered quietly. God had touched her through prayer.

When there is no one to turn to . . .
    LOOK UP
When there is no where else to go . . .
    LOOK UP
When darkness and fears overwhelm you . . .
    LOOK UP, LOOK UP, LOOK UP!
He's as close as a prayer.

• • • • •
LIVE IT OUT!

Can you think of someone who needs *you* to pray for them?

_____

Be willing to lead others in prayer. Even practice by role-playing how you would pray with them. You'll never know how bad some people want to pray and just can't or don't know how! So don't be embarrassed. Praying for people could change their lives—and yours! Read Psalms 5, 38, and 40 for added motivation.

By the way, three years later, my friend is a healthy, hope-filled Christian—and is now helping others.

_____

Let's Do Lunch

"Beck, let's do lunch!"

I'm always checking my calendar and blocking out time to meet and eat. It's one of my favorite things to do. I like to be with people—sharing ideas and feelings, asking advice. And with some people, I can even talk about my problems, disappointments, and hurts.

That's how I got the idea to have an appointment with God. I always had time—or made time—to meet with people for an hour over a meal, so why couldn't I do the same with God? Why did my time with God always get pushed aside, bumped to the end of the day, or put on tomorrow's to-do list?

One day an embarrassing thought struck me: *No one knows me better or loves me more than God, so why is he the one person I squeeze out of my day?* Unable to answer my question, I began to realize my priorities did not reflect my desires.

So I made a simple but very important decision: I would make an appointment with God every day for the rest of my life. I would find a quiet place where God and I would not be interrupted, and I would bring my Bible, pencil, and paper to jot down notes about our conversation.

Once I made that decision, it was no longer a question of if—just when. Now each day I look at my calendar for today's appointment, and I also block out *tomorrow's* slot for my quiet time with God. When that time comes, I read. He speaks. I listen. I write. He listens. We communicate through the Word and through his Spirit.

Now, many years later, my priorities are beginning to reflect my heart's desires—to know and love God better. And there's no better way to get to know a person better than to spend time with him every day! Oh yeah—my time with God did cost me something: a little less TV and a little less sleep.

• • • • •

LIVE IT OUT!

When's the last time you "did lunch" with God? If you were to meet with God daily, when would be the best time? _____

_____

If you were to meet with God daily, what would be a realistic amount of time to spend with him in prayer and Bible reading? ____

If you want to make a decision to have an appointment with God every day, just write a note to him now: _____

_____

_____

Commercial break: *Quietimes Student Prayer Notebook* (Thomas Nelson, 1990), the quiet time notebook I designed for students, is a great tool for your own daily appointment with God. It keeps you accountable to your meeting times and provides a place to write your prayers daily and record God's answers. See the last page in this book if you are interested in keeping your own prayer notebook. Now, back to our regularly scheduled devotional.

The "Write" Way To Pray

I tried *everything* before I came to the conclusion that *writing* my prayers (or conversations) to God was the most effective way for me to talk to him without . . .

falling asleep
getting bored
being distracted
feeling rushed or
forgetting to pray altogether!

Writing down my prayers is what I need to perk up my conversations with God. It's something like "Dear Diary," except that I express my thoughts, feelings, concerns, doubts, requests, and thanks to *God* rather than to myself.

In *Quietimes Student Prayer Notebook*, I've divided up my prayers into four PARTs:

PRAISE
ADMIT
REQUEST and
THANKS.

I call it my PART of prayer because I know that God has a part of prayer, too: speaking to me to me through his Word while I listen.

First, I write to God with words of *praise* for who he is. Then I *admit* to him where I've missed the mark. Next, I *request* God's help in specific areas. And finally, I end my time of written prayer with a personal note of *thanks* to him! By the end of my appointment, I feel like I've really prayed—the "write" way! Maybe you'd like to try it.

• • • • •
LIVE IT OUT!

Try writing your own prayer using the PART pattern.

Dear God, let me begin by praising you. You are terrific! I love you and here's what I really appreciate about you:

_____

_____

_____

I've made some mistakes lately, and I need your help to change. (Read Psalm 139:23–24 and 1 John 1:9.) Please forgive me for:

_____

_____

_____

As usual, I have some special requests to make (I'll try to be open to *whatever* answer you may give), and some special people that I want to pray for:

_____

_____

_____

Thanks for listening, Lord. And thanks, too, for:

_____

_____

_____. I love you.

God, Are You There?

Pam rushed up to me one Sunday morning. "I just *have* to tell you something!" I had no idea what she was going to say, but she sure was excited.

She had recently signed up to audition for a role in a play. When she arrived at the audition, however, she was told she would have to sing! Though she was a good singer, she thought she was only trying out for speaking parts. Panic-stricken, she grew nauseated and wanted to leave.

But then a thought crossed her mind: *God, I haven't been close to you lately, but would you help me? Are you even there?* She soon felt a distinct peace she had not felt before her prayer. The tryout went so well that she was chosen for a solo part in the play!

"It may not seem like a big deal to you, Becky," she told me, "but God showed me that he really cares about me. He's there. Now I know he's listening to my prayers."

Have you been wondering if God is there?

• • • • •
LIVE IT OUT!

Take a few moments now and just talk to God. If you feel like he doesn't even hear your prayers, talk to him about that. He *is* there for you. Read John 14, Psalm 38:9, and Psalm 34:4–8.

LIVING in Relationship WITH OTHERS

LIVE IT! *in Your Home*

Is Your Home a Battleground?

When I was in high school, my home felt like a bomb waiting to explode—every day! Screaming, hollering, and constant fighting were our normal patterns of communicating. I hated to come home from school. And I eventually hated my parents.

Does your home ever sound like this:

"Get off the phone!" (Sis)

"Clean your room!" (Mom)

"Quit borrowing my stuff!" (Bro)

"Can I have the keys?" (You)

"Why only 'til midnight?" (You)

"You *still* haven't taken out the trash?" (Dad)

Family members can drive us crazy in a million ways—and vice versa. We know *just* what to say, what lousy look to give, or how to avoid interrogations. Then, inevitably, the explosion comes!

Honestly, I look back and wonder if *anyone* could have saved my family from growing apart. That's why this section of *Live It!* is so important to me. If even a few of you read this and find encouragement, my difficult struggles will have been worth it.

What are three issues that cause regular battles in your home?

1. _____

2. _____

3. _____

Sometimes it's the timing that ticks someone off; other times it's the tone of voice. What could you do in each of the above situations to relieve the tension *before* the blow-up?

1. _____

2. _____

3. _____

Being part of a family means living *with* people. It's totally different than knowing, liking, and being with friends, because we can't choose our family. Living with our family can include conflict, confrontation, inconvenience, and sacrifice.

Here's a thought to consider: It's not so much *what* happens, but *how you react to it* that can make or break a day in the life of your family.

• • • • •
LIVE IT OUT!

Take a look at some "Preventative Proverbs" for your home and circle the one that stands out the most:

Proverbs 13:3
Proverbs 14:29
Proverbs 15:20
Proverbs 16:32
Proverbs 17:14
Proverbs 18:21
Proverbs 19:13
Proverbs 20:11
Proverbs 21:23

Sinners, Too!

Somewhere between the ages of twelve and twenty-two, our grand expectations of Mom and Dad get shattered in the following areas:

- allowance
- tuition
- vacations
- clothes
- spending money
- a car
- eternal even temper and good moods
- quick forgiveness
- understanding
- leniency of curfew.

But if we look closer at a day in the life of Mom and Dad, we might see:

- a struggle to pay the bills
- a bad day at work
- the difficulty of being a single parent
- a hot temper
- their own childhood traumas
- personality flaws
- inability to understand the "generation gap"
- unfulfilled expectations they've had for their kids!

I don't know how or when it happens, but one day you look up and notice that your parents are sinners, too. They're not perfect. They need God. They need money. They need love, forgiveness, maybe even a break from taking care of you.

Colossians 3:12–14 has great advice for the person who wants to be an understanding family member: "Clothe yourself with [or let your outer appearance be] compassion, kindness, humility, gentleness, and patience. Bear with each other and forgive *whatever* grievances you may have against one another. *Forgive as the Lord forgave you. . . . put on love."*

• • • • •
LIVE IT OUT!

Which characteristic listed in Colossians 3:12–14 do you show the *most* to your parents? _____

The *least*? _____

Now, make a real effort to change this one characteristic and "clothe yourself" in one of the attitudes or actions from Colossians this week!

Take a shot at memorizing Colossians 3:12–14.

Home of the Brave

The phone rang, and Ken answered it.

"Hey, Ken—we wanna go to the drive-in tonight, but none of us can get the car. What do you think, can you drive?"

A relatively new Christian, Ken found himself in a tight situation. He knew there were two ways to ask for the car:

1. Tell the truth and be told no.

2. Lie and be assured the keys to the car.

Before becoming a Christian, he had regularly lied to his parents. It just seemed easier. Now, instead of doing what he knew was right, he impulsively chose to lie, thinking that this one time wouldn't matter.

Well, it *did* matter. When his dad caught him in the lie, he said to Ken, "So, is that what you've been learning at church?" Now Ken not only had proven himself untrustworthy, but he had also tarnished his Christian image.

Being a Christian in a non-Christian home certainly has its moments of glory—and defeat! Actually, being a Christian in any setting can be tough, but most will agree that in the home, people see the real you. Once you've told your family you're a Christian, they begin to watch carefully the language you choose, the respect you show, and your willingness to obey the rules. All of these are outside indicators of what's happened inside you.

"Walking your talk" is especially important in your home. Each member of your family knew you before you met Christ. Showing them a changed person with a new set of standards for life can open the door for Jesus Christ to come into your home. Will you let him use you?

If you are looking for practical ways to show Christ's presence in your home, try these:

Honor your parents. Simply show them respect (Ephesians 6:1–3).

Be at peace, as often as possible. Don't raise your voice to your parents. Yelling may or may not be a habit of yours, but do all that you can to control your temper (Proverbs 18:6, 17:9).

Let your actions match your words. This may be the key to leading your parents to Christ. Be willing to make some sacrifices for their salvation.

• • • • •

LIVE IT OUT!

What three attitudes, actions, or areas could you focus on that, over time, would reflect Christ's presence in your life?

1. _____

2. _____

3. _____

What changes do you need to make in each of these areas?

1. _____

2. _____

3. _____

Begin each morning this week with a prayer (and a conscious effort) to work on these three areas. Did your parents notice?

Changing Homes

Stepfathers. Divorce. Half-sisters. Single-parent homes. Adultery. Affairs. Living with Mom's boyfriend. Third marriages. Separation.

Many high schoolers live in "changing homes" these days. Though some live in better situations than others, I haven't met a student yet who doesn't struggle with a changing home life. It's difficult to know what to say to these students, because there are no perfect solutions or snappy answers to help them cope with a changing home.

At a camp recently, I was asked to pray with a junior high girl who was nearly suicidal because her parents were getting divorced. At another youth group, a disgusted student said, "All I ever do is babysit my stepbrother. I have no social life." And at a public school assembly, a girl told me her stepfather had asked her—*and* her girlfriend—to sleep with him! Sadly, that's happening in America today.

What can you do to cope with the pain, frustration, and disillusionment of a changing home?

First, *pray.* Pray for your parents and their relationship. Pray for God to be real in their lives. Remember that *some* separations don't automatically lead to divorce; that *some* parents who divorce remarry into better situations; and that *some* marital problems can lead people right to Jesus!

Pray daily and diligently for your own attitudes and actions in the home. It's easy to get bitter or downright rebellious toward a new stepparent. Pray for strength to handle your emotions.

Second, *don't be afraid to see a Christian counselor.* Divorce not only affects your parents, it affects you, too. Get Christian counsel with your family or on your own—especially if you find that your grades are dropping, your friendships are changing, or your feelings (such as depression or anger or rebellion) are becoming more than you can handle.

It is important to express your true *feelings* during this difficult time and to receive comfort and advice from a Christian professional. In fact, if physical abuse is occurring in your home, I want to emphasize that you *must* see a counselor for your own help and protection. He or she can guide you through the necessary steps for helping yourself and your family members. Taking this scary step will not be easy, but it is essential.

Third, *work on your own spiritual growth through reading your Bible, going to church, and spending time with Christian friends.* Through God's Word and a caring Christian community, you will find comfort, hope, and eventually healing (Colossians 3).

Fourth, *don't give up on the possibility of a successful marriage for yourself in the future.* Often people react to their parents' failed marriage by (1) refusing to marry, (2) just living together with someone, or (3) getting married, but expecting it to end in divorce. These options are not God's best. Remember, when marriage is entered into and honored in God's way, it takes a lot of effort, but it works (Hebrews 13:4)!

• • • • •

LIVE IT OUT!

If any of these thoughts have hit home for you, begin now with a prayer for your parents, for your current situation, and for God's intervention in all of your lives.

A Kiss and a Prayer

When I was little, my mom and I used to say prayers together every night before I went to bed. I can't remember when we stopped, but I wish we hadn't.

As I got older, our personalities clashed daily. Little disagreements turned into big blowouts. We found it increasingly difficult to say anything nice to each other. The situation worsened to the point where I would tell my mom I hated her. And at age seventeen, leaving home altogether seemed my only option.

The years of reacting and rebelling against my parents took their toll. But when *I* became a parent, the whole picture changed! Remembering how I "lost it" with my mom made me look hard for ways to stay close to my son, Jake. I decided on a kiss and a prayer each night:

"G'night, Jake."
"G'night, Mom."
(SMOOCH)
"Let's say prayers, honey."
"Okay, Mom, you start."

At the end of our bedtime ritual, I tuck Jake in, turn off the light and tiptoe out of the room.

No matter *what* the day has been like, we end every night with a kiss and a prayer. We add little apologies and hugs whenever needed, so that the sun never goes down on our anger (Ephesians 4:26). It's a good, peaceful feeling.

LIVE IT OUT!

When's the last time you had a "kiss and a prayer" with your parents? It may sound childlike, but try this:

Tonight, before you head for your bedroom, head for your parents' room. Ask them if you could pray out loud together. Some families might already do this, but if yours doesn't, try it anyway! See how creative you can be. Offer to kneel by their bed, or by the couch. Maybe you'll be able to revive the kiss-and-a-prayer ritual in your home!

Taking a Good Thing for Granted

The other evening my husband took Jake on an all-night fishing trip. I remember thinking, *Great—I'll have some peace and quiet so I can get a lot of things done!* I waved good-bye from the doorstep and went inside, trying to decide which project to tackle first.

The house seemed awfully quiet—too quiet, in fact, so I turned on the TV for company. But every channel was more boring than the next. I found myself wandering aimlessly around the house, not wanting to do anything. What I really wanted was someone to talk to!

Then a thought crossed my mind: *What if they never came home? I would be so lonely.*

I reflected on how I'd been relating to Jake during the past few weeks. He's at that age when he asks millions of questions about everything, and I had been bothered and irritated. Now, after only two hours alone, here I was, missing him!

Waiting for them to come home was terrible. I began to realize that I had taken for granted the people who meant the most to me. I hadn't stopped to appreciate all they had to offer:

• They *liked* to be with me.

• I could always count on hugs from them . . . even if I had to ask sometimes.

• They were always willing to listen to my stories of the day.

I really had been taking a good thing for granted. It reminded me of a high schooler who once told me her parents paid her five dollars a day simply to *talk* to them. She had so resisted sharing her day's events with Mom and Dad each day after school that they resorted to this extreme (and costly) solution!

However bad or good our family circumstances may be, it's easy to wish for something more or someone better. But, if they were all gone tomorrow—no one to talk with, no one to provide for us, no one to need us—would our perspective change?

I'm sure it would! It's a matter of looking at the same old family in a whole new way.

When my "boys" walked in the door the following day, I hugged them, kissed them, hugged them, didn't nag them about their smelly, fishy clothes, and told them again and again how much I had missed them!

They stood there looking at me, bewildered. "Is anything wrong?" they asked. "Are you feeling okay? Did you get too much sun?"

"No," I said, "I just couldn't wait for you to get home. You're my family."

• • • • •

LIVE IT OUT!

Blow your parents away today:

1. Tell them something you appreciate about them.
2. Give them *both* a hug.
3. Thank them for something they've recently done for you.

4. Offer to help them out with something.
5. Say to each member of your family, "I love you!"

Last Laughs

I grew up in a home where Mom yelled at Dad, Mom and Dad yelled at the kids, the kids yelled at each other—and the neighbors heard everything!

Now I have my own home. And one day I started yelling at my husband, Roger. He said, "Becky, forget it. We're not going to have a yelling home. We're not going to say things that hurt, or things we'll regret. We're not going to call each other names like 'stupid' or worse."

We did real well . . . for two days. Then I got mad again. We quickly realized that if we weren't going to yell and scream and fuss, we'd have to do something else. So, Rog came up with an idea: We would hold hands when we fought!

Right.

I didn't want to hold hands. I wanted to be mad. So I walked away. And he came after me. I ran into another room, still mad. He continued to chase. By the time he caught up with me and grabbed my hand, I had forgotten what I was so upset about. We started to laugh. Roll on the floor. Cry. Laugh.

It worked! You can't yell, much less be mad, at someone who is holding your hands!

We made it a family goal to hold hands and be gentle when we are mad. It's an effective way to extinguish the big blazes quickly!

● ● ● ● ●
LIVE IT OUT!

1. Call a family council meeting and discuss the above idea as a way to break the ice during a difficult situation at home. If you prefer to come up with something better, great.

2. Copy Proverbs 15:1 on a piece of paper and place it on the refrigerator door for all to see—and memorize.

LIVE IT! with Friends

In Search of a True Friend

Often students will say to me, "I don't really have a true friend." They'll tell me how they've been hurt or disappointed or jilted by supposed friends. Those kinds of things happen to all of us at times. True friends, on the other hand, possess certain qualities that make them more special. But before you search for *someone else* with these qualities, it's worth it to search yourself first:

Are You a True Friend?

	Do You?		Do They?	
	Y	**N**	**Y**	**N**
1. Do you keep secrets confidential (Proverbs 16:28)?	☐	☐	☐	☐
2. Do you give them good advice and positive criticism in a way that encourages and helps rather than hurts or demeans (Ephesians 4:29)?	☐	☐	☐	☐
3. Do you always treat them kindly rather than rudely—just because they are your close friends (1 Corinthians 13:4)?	☐	☐	☐	☐

	Do You?		Do They?	
	Y	**N**	**Y**	**N**
4. Do you consistently keep your promises to them (Psalm 15, especially v. 4)?	☐	☐	☐	☐
5. Are you loyal to them, even when they're not around (1 Corinthians 13:4–6, *Living Bible*)?	☐	☐	☐	☐

● ● ● ●
LIVE IT OUT!

If you haven't already, look up the Scripture passages listed above and identify the friendship area you could improve the most. (A thought to consider: The dictionary defines friendship as "intimacy based on mutual esteem and kindness.") How will you improve your friendship qualities in this area? _____

_____

_____

Rejection—the Silent Killer

We had been best friends for a long time. Then, all of a sudden, she wouldn't talk to me, look at me, or return my phone calls! I wasn't even sure what I had done to make her so mad. I felt angry, helpless, hurt, and most of all, rejected. Each night I paced back and forth by the phone, hoping something might change, hoping she would call.

She never did. And I felt a real sense of loss over someone with whom I had spent a lot of time and shared great memories.

Sound familiar? I can name at least five more friendships in junior and senior high that ended in that same way—total silence.

As a former coach, youth worker, and now a youth speaker, I always hear of similar endings to relationships. I want to offer you hope, and give a few suggestions to help you feel less rejected by the silent treatment. When you encounter rejection, take these four steps:

> *Admit* any fault of your own,
> *Apologize* in person, or
> *Attempt* to reconcile your relationship in some other way (a letter, for example), and
> *Ask for help* from God *and* from others.

If you give *each* of these steps your sincere effort, you have a very good chance to reconcile your relationship. (There are exceptions, of course, such as when a friend has severe family problems, or when parents restrict you from seeing or talking to an old friend.) Just remember that healing may take time.

● ● ● ● ●
LIVE IT OUT!

If you're currently experiencing rejection from a friend, try the above four steps as follows:

Admit: Think about your part in the problem. Rarely is a fight or argument only one person's fault. What might you have done or said to initiate this silence?

Apologize: Are you willing to confess your part in the disagreement and apologize for it? (You do not need to take responsibility for what you did *not* do or say, but you must be willing to humble yourself for your contribution to the problem.)

Attempt: If they still refuse to talk or call, write a letter that includes any necessary apology, your honest feelings about the person, and your desire to be friends again. Then either mail it or give it to them in person. Often a letter is less threatening and gives the person time to understand your side of the situation. But be *very* careful that the tone of your letter is not hurtful or cynical—you'll only make matters worse!

Ask for help: If you are really distraught and nothing else has worked so far, perhaps you can ask a parent, teacher, or some other trustworthy friend (preferably older) to meet with the two of you and help bring healing to your relationship.

Finally, read these Scriptures for extra encouragement: Matthew 5:23–24; Colossians 3:12-14; Matthew 5:9.

Forget Me Not

When she walked into the youth group meeting for the first time, every head turned. She was thin, pretty, and dressed like a model. Many students in the room made a point of welcoming her and getting to know her.

When a nerdy-looking guy entered the room a couple of minutes later, people hardly noticed. His clothes were tacky and his hairstyle outdated. Only the youth director bothered to say hello to him.

As the meeting got started, everyone sat with their usual friends. Many asked the new girl to sit with them, but not even one of the "regulars" approached the new guy to sit with him. He was different. He took a seat in the back of the room.

When first-timers were introduced, the new girl, Janine, stood up, told her name and her grade, and then thanked everyone for how welcome they had made her feel. The room filled with applause.

Then the new guy stood up in back. "My name is Phil," he said. "I just want you to know I don't feel welcome at all. No one has even talked to me." Then he sat down.

The room suddenly fell silent.

After a few extremely awkward moments had passed, the youth director broke the silence. "Okay, let's talk about what just happened. First, I want you to know that Phil and Janine are both friends of mine. They go to another church, but I asked them to come here tonight. I asked Phil to dress like a nerd and Janine to dress cool. The whole thing was a setup.

"I'm sorry to say," he continued, "that our youth group fell right into the trap of paying attention to the popular-looking student and totally ignoring the not-so-popular-looking student. Why don't we spend the rest of our meeting tonight talking about how we can be more open, friendly, and Christlike to people we don't know—no matter how they look or what they wear."

● ● ● ● ●
LIVE IT OUT!

1. Who did you relate to most as you read this story? Janine? Phil? The youth group regulars? _____

2. If you are in a youth group, how does your group (on the whole) treat first-timers? _____

_____

3. How do *you* meet and treat people you don't know very well? _____

_____

4. What is one way that you can help your group to accept and welcome new friends? _____

_____

5. Take a look at Matthew 25:31–46 and James 2:1–12. If you applied these passages to your present attitude toward meeting new people, what would you have to change? _____

_____

Are Your Companions Cool—or Fools?

When I was in junior high, cheerleading, synchronized swimming, field hockey, and basketball kept me surrounded by friends who did and liked the same "cool" things that I did—sports, competition, and performance. At that time in my life, I couldn't have been happier.

But when I started high school, my definition of "cool" began to change. All those sports teams and extracurricular activities seemed to take time away from a new set of friends I was making. I grew more interested in being popular and fitting in with a group of older kids who liked to party.

My sports commitments prevented me from being home after school to talk on the phone, make plans for the weekend, or drive around. I became so afraid I'd miss out on my time with those friends that I began to consider dropping sports. As it turned out, the pressure within me to be popular was stronger than my desire to pursue athletic goals. Though I remained a cheerleader, I quit all my sports teams to spend more time with my new friends.

My previous friendships began to fall apart, but I didn't care—I was making new ones. By the middle of my first year of high school, I was constantly hanging out with nonathletic, upperclass party-types—and by the end of the year had become a regular user of cigarettes and drugs, and a colossal beer drinker.

Looking back, I can see that the entire course of my life changed *when I changed my friends*. My desire to hang out with people who *appeared* to be more fun, more exciting, and more popular ended up destroying the person I was truly meant to be in high school. In fact, I never even graduated with my original class; I finished up a year early to get away from all the strained and hateful relationships. And I left behind many unfulfilled dreams for those years.

• • • • •
LIVE IT OUT!

Take a serious look at who you are (intellectual, theatrical, athletic, quiet, outgoing, musical, etc.) and what you believe you were meant to be and do in school (cheerleading, orchestra or band, student council, sports, perhaps none of the above). Then *honestly* ask yourself a few questions:

1. Are my current friends the best for me?
2. Do they cause me to compromise my faith?
3. Do they encourage me in my talents?
4. Do I fight with them over how I spend my time?
5. Do my parents like my friends?

Years later, I still deeply regret not listening to the warnings of my parents, coaches, or teachers about my friendships. Could these questions be a warning to you?
How? _____

Copy Proverbs 13:20 below. How does it apply to your life right now? _____

_____

_____

_____

Say It!

I wanted her to know. We had been the best of party buddies in high school and I hadn't seen her since my recent conversion to

Christ. I had experienced so many exciting changes, and I was dying to tell her.

But how? We had never talked about God before. She'd think I was really off the wall!

Have you ever been in this dilemma? Look at these words from a song by Kim Boyce entitled "Say It":

> Say it
> They will know it's true
> Say it
> They'll see the love in you.
>
> Now you ask me how to tell them
> That you really love Him
> And if they don't believe?
>
> Say what He's done for you
> Tell 'em that your heart is new
> He'll give you the words
> So please
> Say it! Say it! Say it![1]

• • • • •
LIVE IT OUT!

Often the most effective way to talk to someone about Jesus is to describe him as your friend.

Give them examples of ways he has helped you, advice he has given you, and the benefits of experiencing his forgiveness (1 John 1:9). Share how you talk to him about everything in prayer (Philippians 4:6–7, James 4:2). Explain why you asked him into your life (using Romans 3:23, for example), and give examples that show how knowing him has made a difference in your life.

You might even share with them that because you love your friend Jesus and are loyal to him, you will do some things

[1]"Say It" by Kim Boyce and Brian Tankersley. © 1988 by Word Music and Promiseland Music (both divisions of Word, Inc.). All rights reserved. International copyright secured. Used by permission.

differently than you used to (John 15). And finally, be willing to introduce your friend (and Lord) Jesus to them. If they aren't very interested now, don't feel bad. As they watch your life change, they may very well begin to ask *you* about your new friend!

Is there anyone you would like to "say it" to? _____

From Total Respect to Total Disappointment

Jerece had been really close with her older sister—you could say they were best friends. She almost idolized Pamela—she wanted to dress like her, be like her, go to the same college she did. They shared every secret and every experience.

While in high school, Jerece attended a Campus Life meeting and loved it. After four or five weeks, she felt the desire to ask Christ into her life. When she called Pamela at college to tell her, she thought she heard something distant in Pamela's voice, but didn't think too much of it.

Finally the school year ended, and Jerece looked forward to having her sister back at home again for the summer. Now she would be able to share with Pamela all about her first year of high school—classes, new friends, dating, and especially becoming a Christian!

Pamela couldn't have cared less. And Jerece was devastated. It tore her apart to think that her best friend wouldn't want to know about her life, especially her new relationship with Christ. What was worse, Jerece could tell that Pamela had grown a lot more wild than she had ever been before.

The secrets they had once shared were no more. And as they headed into the next school year, Jerece felt angry, betrayed, and disillusioned—by her sister and by God. She just couldn't stop loving God. But she couldn't stop loving her sister, either.

Over the next year, Jerece began to grow in her relationship with God, attending church and Bible study and maturing in her faith. She began to realize that that the choices she needed to make and the people she needed to respect and imitate as a Christian might not include her older sister. It was a tough step to take, but Jerece knew she needed to take it.

As Jerece's faith became a strong, solid, confident part of *her* life, her relationship with Pamela gradually turned around a few years later. In fact, because of Jerece's example (and her invitations), Pamela began to attend church and discover for herself why Jerece had become a follower of Jesus!

● ● ● ● ●
LIVE IT OUT!

Can you identify with this story in any way? How? _____

_____

_____

Many students face rejection for their faith on the home front or with friends. If you were—or are—facing such a circumstance, how would you handle it? _____

_____

_____

Read the following verses to boost your confidence: Philemon 6; 1 Thessalonians 4:11–12.

Just One!

Dawson Trotman was an incredible man whose philosophy of life was "to know Christ and to make him known."

He believed that students had the ability to make a difference in their world for Christ. So he founded a ministry called the Navigators, which emphasized leading one person to Christ and discipling them in the ways of the Lord. Then, each of those "disciples" would lead one person to Christ and disciple that person. So each person's goal as a Christian was to "reproduce" eventually.

Dawson was remarkable in his desire to lead people to Christ and help them grow strong in their faith. He even modeled the principle of laying down his life for others when he drowned while rescuing another person.

In a booklet called *Born to Reproduce*, Dawson shared some of his thoughts on how students can reach "just one" for Christ: "When all things are right between you and the Lord, regardless of how much or how little you may know intellectually from the standpoint of the world, you can be a spiritual parent. And that, incidentally, may even be when you are very young in the Lord. . . . Are you producing? If not, why not? Is it because of a lack of communion with Christ . . . ? Or is it some sin in your life, an unconfessed something, that has stopped the flow? Or is it that you are still a babe?" (Dawson then quotes Hebrews 5:12: "Though by this time you ought to be teachers, you need someone to teach you the elementary truths of God's word all over again.")

How can you make Christ known, or perhaps even be a spiritual parent to a friend—especially if you're not an outgoing person? Dawson Trotman would tell you to begin with *one* person. Can you think of one person in your school—in one of your classes or on your sports team—that you could:

Invest your time in?

Invite to join you in a Bible study?

Involve in your church or youth group? And eventually, Infiltrate your school with, making Christ known to two more friends?

• • • • •
LIVE IT OUT!

Write the name of that one person here: _____

Read the following passages for encouragement: 2 Timothy 2:2; Hebrews 5:12; 1 Peter 2:2–3.

Today, ask yourself, Am I growing in my knowledge of Christ and am I making him known? (Answer honestly!) _____

If you'd like to read more about Dawson Trotman, you can purchase a little booklet at most Christian bookstores called *Born to Reproduce*, published by NavPress. I'd encourage you to get a copy!

LIVE IT! *on Your Dates*

Temptation Eyes

At a summer high school camp I met a great gal, Laura. She was a doll—fun-loving and always happy. Her smile, pretty eyes, and cute cheerleader shape made her appear all "together."

She *seemed* to be an on-fire Christian, but as the week progressed, she began to tell me more and more about her personal life. She shared with me one very strong temptation she had—to have sex with her boyfriend. Though she knew it was wrong and truly felt bad about it, she couldn't seem to go out with him and *not* have a physical relationship.

"Becky," she confided, "I just can't seem to say no."

It takes a lot of strength to
   look the other way,
     ignore,
       flee from, and
         avoid sexual temptation.

Believe it or not, God knows and understands that our lives are surrounded by temptation. First Corinthians 10:13 says, "No temptation has seized you except what is common to man. And God is faithful; he will not let you be tempted beyond what you can bear. But when you are tempted, he will also provide a way out so that you can stand up under it."

Passion, lust, adultery, permissiveness, even perversity aren't exclusive traits of our generation. Both the Old and New Testaments of the Bible are full of such stories. Ever since Adam and Eve, sexual temptation seems to be lurking around every corner.

"How can a young man [or woman] keep his [or her] way pure?" David asks God in Psalm 119:9. Then he answers his own question: "By living according to your word."

Laura has stayed in touch with me since camp. She has become accountable to an older Christian, and we both agree that making decisions about dating has to be according to God's Word. It is the very best place for students to learn how to keep their way pure!

• • • • •
LIVE IT OUT!

From the list below, which Scripture passage most "hits home" for you? Why? Take some time to think about where you've been and where you're going.

	What does it say?	*How am I doing?*
1 Thessalonians 4:3–8		
Philippians 1:9–11		
2 Timothy 2:22		
Proverbs 22:1		
Proverbs 24:6		

Love in the '90s

Cara fell in love with Tim about a year ago. I didn't see her as much at church, and when we did see each other, we weren't able to talk like we used to. She wouldn't open up. I had a feeling something wasn't right.

Then, a few weeks ago, I got a call.

"Becky, Cara really wants to talk to you, but she's afraid."

"Why?" I said.

There was a pause. "You haven't heard? Cara's pregnant."

Cara and I met for dinner a few days later. For a while, we both felt quite awkward. Finally I mustered the courage to break the ice. Though I wanted to say, "Cara, what's really going on in your life?" instead I asked, "So, how're you doing?"

"Okay, I guess."

Then the story unfolded. We talked about her parents' divorce years ago, the lack of love in her family, and how Tim's "love" *seemed* to fill the need her family didn't meet. As a result of their unrestrained intimacy, Cara, at nineteen, was now facing a devastating set of consequences. She was definitely a Christian, and had known what God's Word said about sex outside of marriage. Now she was pregnant. My heart ached for her.

Cara went on with her story. On the morning she had planned to get an abortion, her best friend had called Cara's mother (who didn't know that Cara was pregnant), hoping to get her to convince Cara to change her mind. Her mother immediately confronted Cara about the pregnancy and begged her to discuss the options available to her and her baby—other than abortion.

Now five-and-a-half months pregnant, Cara is making plans to put up her baby for adoption. "The decisions I face now are so overwhelming," she told me. "I wonder what I'll face in a year or in ten years just because I didn't follow God's Word."

Now she's working through the process of forgiving herself—and others. She's also learning to accept *God's* forgiveness of her.

"Finding forgiveness has been really helpful," she said, "but, I really learned this one the hard way. I was so naive to think it couldn't happen to me."

• • • • •

LIVE IT OUT!

Some students may define *love* as sexual intimacy, but that's *not* God's definition of love.

What is *your* definition of love? _____

_____

What are your standards regarding sex and marriage? (See 1 Corinthians 6:13–20; Romans 13:13–14; 1 Thessalonians 4:3–5; Hebrews 13:4.) _____

_____

If you are in a compromising situation right now, do something about it immediately—talk to a pastor, Christian counselor, friend, parent, or teacher. *Please* don't wait until it's too late! The *momentary* humiliation in reaching out for help is nothing compared to a *lifetime* of consequences.

Saying No

Maybe you've seen it before:
The wink. The raised eyebrows.
The hug or pinch or sexy smile.

Maybe you've heard it before:
"If you loved me, you would . . ."
"This is how you can show me you love me . . ."
"Someday we'll get married . . ."

The list goes on.
And so does the list of
    broken hearts,
        shattered dreams,
            empty promises.

Saying no means abstaining from sex before marriage. It is God's way to help you avoid
- unwanted pregnancy,
- immorality,
- guilt over sex sin.

Saying no means
- putting up with jokes about being a prude,
- allowing people to call you naive or old-fashioned,
- risking the loss of a relationship,
- rejecting "progressive" sex education

Saying no means
- respecting yourself,
- earning respect from others (lots of it),
- saving yourself for *one* lifetime partner,
- marrying pure,
- living *with* responsibility and *without* guilt
- enjoying a right relationship with God.

Saying no means
- being a leader, not a follower,
- having and holding on to strong Christian values,
- having values to pass on to your kids!

Saying no means
- actively choosing to wait until marriage!

● ● ● ● ●

LIVE IT OUT!

Look up these Scriptures and rephrase them in your own words:

Ephesians 4:17–19 _____

_____

Colossians 3:1–5 _____

_____

1 Thessalonians 4:3–8 _____

_____

Where do *you* stand when it comes to saying no? _____

_____

Have you made a decision to abstain from sex until marriage? Why or why not? _____

_____

Are You Hot?

My coed Bible study began with a few chuckles, a couple of squirms, and more than a few whispers. The topic? Love, sex, and dating.

"What is love?" I asked as an opener. "How can you know if you love someone?"

After a few comments, we moved right to the issue of dating. I suggested we look at a few Scriptures and ask how these verses apply to dating. We hadn't even made it through the first passage when I knew we were in trouble.

Ephesians 5:1–7 created an uproar, especially when we got to verse 3: "But among you there must not be even a *hint* of sexual immorality."

"What exactly is immorality, anyway?" one student asked.

"And what's *sexual* immorality?" another added.

Then the clincher: "Just how much is a *hint*?"

I sat back in my chair and realized this was no passive bunch. They were not in the least bit thrilled to hear what God's Word had to say about sex and the single student. In fact, their greatest concern was not "Where should I draw the line?" but "Just tell me how far I can go and still be okay."

Actually, we laughed a lot that Monday night at Bible study.

But I pressed on, uncovering more Scripture. I even got out a dictionary to look up the definitions of "hint," "sexual," and "immorality"—only to add to their groans and growing disillusionment!

Finally I said, "Hey, you guys. You read the Bible, don't you? Haven't you seen these Scriptures before?"

Then an unforgettable line tumbled out of Eugene's mouth. With utter sincerity he said, in true California style, "Like, Becky, this could change my whole lifestyle!"

With a smile and the same total sincerity, I looked at my table of eight high schoolers and said, "Like, you guys, it's supposed to!"

We all cracked up laughing—but reality had hit home!

God gave us his guidelines on love, sex, and dating not to steal our fun or make our single years boring, but to protect us and provide for us.

It seemed a tough pill for the group to swallow. But now that the truth was out, it was time to dig deeper into the Word and into our personal convictions and standards. We weren't done yet.

And next Monday's Bible study would be on the same topic!

• • • • •

LIVE IT OUT!

Look up each verse listed below and comment on how you think it relates to love, sex, dating—and most of all—you. Share it with a friend—maybe even the one you are dating!

Philippians 1:9–11 _____

_____

Philippians 2:3–4 _____

_____

Romans 12:1–2 _____

Is It True Love?

Tina wanted to know if her feeling was true love. She was always thinking about him—though it seemed he didn't think about her nearly as much. She could feel physically sick over not hearing from him, and when she saw him, her heart actually pounded faster and louder.

She finally cornered me. "Becky, what's the difference between love and infatuation?"

We came to the conclusion that infatuation was a ton of feelings, sparked by physical attraction and evidenced by tingles, chills, goose bumps, hot flashes, and sweaty hands!

Then what was love?

As a new Christian, I had wondered the same·thing as Tina when I was dating. Of all the stories, conversations, and advice I heard on the subject, one unforgettable example stood out as a test of true love: 1 Corinthians 13.

I can evaluate my "love" by reading verses 4 through 7 (*Living Bible*):

> Love is very patient (uh, oh)
> and kind,
> never jealous or envious (oh, my goodness),
> never boastful or proud (oh no),
> never haughty
> or selfish
> or rude (right!). . . .

I challenged Tina to take the True Love Test, basing her "love" for her boyfriend on 1 Corinthians 13. Then I added, using the well-worn phrase, "Remember, Tina, love is *not* a feeling, but a decision!"

If you've got a relationship brewing, take the True Love Test. Open your Bible to 1 Corinthians 13 and ask yourself: Is *your* "love" patient? Kind? Never jealous? Never envious? Never boastful?

Never proud? Never haughty? Never selfish? Never rude? And so on through verse 7.

• • • • •
LIVE IT OUT!

As you read through this passage, which area stands out as the best place to start improving your "love quotient"? How are you going to do it? Be specific.

_____

_____

_____

Cool, Cooler, Totally Cool!

I've seen it work both ways.

The desire for a boyfriend or girlfriend can change a person's values. It's called compromise. It can happen as early as junior high, but high school is often the do-or-die battleground.

First, you check out a potential partner's "package":

Is he or she an athlete?
Cute, gorgeous, or okay?
Popular or not so popular?
Christian, no way a Christian, or you're not sure?
Humorous, intellectual, or both?
Good reputation or not so good?
Older, same age, or younger?

Then you make your move—in other words, you let your feelings be known. You wait for the news to travel—which can mean hours, days, sometimes even painfully slow weeks before the person gets your signals and you know his or her response. If you find the interest is mutual—you're off!

I've seen it happen over and over.

A young and growing Christian begins to date a popular, fun, crazy, non-Christian (i.e. one who has not yet given his or her life to Jesus Christ, even though he or she may attend church). Before long the Christian starts getting . . .

Cool   Drifts away somewhat from youth group, small group Bible study, or church; becomes "too busy" for things that *used* to be important.

Cooler   Slowly quits reading the Bible and can't really get into praying; picks up a few habits of the world; exhibits a shift in priorities. When values and morals are challenged, he or she seems to lack the strength to stand firm.

Totally Cool Begins to compromise—even disown—previously held values and morals; no longer feels comfortable in church; and, depending on how long and how far the person drifts from the Lord, may get involved in sexual immorality, possibly sexually transmitted diseases, sometimes pregnancy, and always heartache.

Honestly, I wouldn't share this if I thought it was the exception. But unfortunately, I see it more as the rule. The kind of person you spend time with and give your affection to (such as someone you are dating) *will* affect your relationship with God. And deep down, you'll know whether the effect is positive or negative. (See Proverbs 13:20.)

LIVE IT OUT!

Ask yourself a serious question: Am I in a **cool** stage, a **cooler** stage, or am I **totally cool** (as described above)?

To get help, start with a prayer to God, remembering that *he* loves you very much and wants the best for you. Perhaps you might ask him for . . .

* forgiveness,
* strength to come back,
* people to help and support you through a transition, and
* patience to wait for the kind of date he would want for you.

Then, take a look at these timely words of advice: Ephesians 4:17–24; Ephesians 5:8–20; 2 Corinthians 6:14–18; Romans 12:1–2.

In His Hands

One couple fell in love at first sight.

Another couple didn't even like their future spouse the first time they met!

One couple had dated for five years—since ninth grade.

One couple dated before, during, and after becoming Christians.

It seems like there's just no simple formula to find the "right one." But everybody wants to. For some unknown reason, the thought always seems to cross your mind when you're dating someone: "Could he be the one? Could she be my future wife?"

Then add this to the mix: The older a girl gets, the more anxious she is about getting married—while the older a guy gets, the less interested he becomes! There are so many variables in the adventure of finding a date for a mate!

Does God have any guidelines? Any clues on how to know when you've found the right one?

My personal conviction is that God has one special person for the Christian to marry. Though not all Christians hold that view, all will agree on the following guidelines for finding the right one:

Do not marry an unbeliever. Plain and simple. (See 2 Corinthians 6:14.)

Seek the advice of your parents. Be willing to listen to their approval or disapproval—it could protect you from heartache in the future. (See Ephesians 6:1–3.)

Ask your Christian friends —especially those who have had a part in your spiritual growth—if they think this relationship is a good one, a healthy one, for both of you. Is it one that brings glory to God? (See Hebrews 13:7.)

Ask yourself if this person is God's best for your life. If there is doubt, hesitancy, or fear about the marriage, be brave enough to cancel the engagement or postpone the wedding date until you are sure. Waiting *now* is *much* better than divorce later!

• • • • •
LIVE IT OUT!

Interview a couple you admire. Ask them to tell their stories—how they met, fell in love, got engaged, and married. Make a list of the things you see in their relationship that you'd like to have as a part of your marriage. Then, (and this truly is a tough part) *be willing to wait* for someone who shares those same dreams and values. Remember, you're waiting for the very best!

If you find it hard to accept the above list of guidelines or don't want to take the time to confirm your relationship through those steps, ask youself this question (and answer honestly): "What's the hurry?"

ROBERT McCOY '89

The Exam Jam

In my senior year, the last week of school was reserved for final exams, and no regular classes met. To celebrate, my friends and I decided to drop in at the local bar for a couple of beers between the morning and afternoon tests. We yucked it up for a while, and then returned for our exams—complete with glassy eyes, loud mouths, and beer breath. Naively I figured my teacher wouldn't notice. But in my carelessness, I arrived late—a definite no-no in finals etiquette.

My chemistry teacher was so angry that she ordered me to take my test into her office and wait for her. After a few minutes, she stomped in and blasted me about my tardiness, my smart mouth, and my disrespect. She made it clear that this was the last straw. I should have taken the moment much more seriously, but my beer-laden brain kept telling me, "Aw, no big deal." After all, school was almost over—what could she do to me?

She left me in her office, where I began to take my test. I can't remember the exact details, but within a few moments I had located a stack of previously taken tests on her desk. Let's just say that I whipped through my chem final in no time flat!

When I turned in my test to Mrs. Goldstein, I gave her the cocky look of one who thought she had beaten—or at least outwitted—her foe. But a week later, when I opened my report card, the look on my face was anything but cocky. Mrs. Goldstein had flunked me!

Although most people consider cheating to be wrong, nearly all students—Christian or not—are tempted by it, and many give in to the temptation. One Scripture passage in particular seems relevant here: "Whoever can be trusted with very little can also be trusted with much, and whoever is dishonest with very little will also be dishonest with much" (Luke 16:10). A person who refuses to cheat—even when many consider it harmless, insignificant, or even normal behavior—has remained honest in a situation that no one else might notice. But Christians have something more to consider: Even though another person may never know, *God* sees us. Do we consider what God thinks of us? Take some time to think about your stand on cheating. And then stand by it!

• • • • •
LIVE IT OUT!

If you knew you would lose a grade by admitting that you had cheated, would you fess up? If you actually have cheated, but weren't caught, what benefits might you experience by turning yourself in? _____

_____

_____

_____

What are your convictions about cheating? Have they stayed the same or changed in the last few years? Why or why not? _____

_____

_____

_____

_____

_____

Mouth Traps

"A gossip betrays a confidence; so avoid a man who talks too much," says Proverbs 20:19. Are you a gossip?

Webster defines gossip as (1) a person who habitually reveals personal or sensational facts, and (2) a rumor or report of a private or intimate nature.

The definition reminds me of the daily conversation in the hall of any junior high school. But in high school, the "sensational facts" of broken relationships, two-timing, lies, and weekend escapades get much more juicy—and tempting to pass along! I call these gossip opportunities "mouth traps."

Is it really possible for a student to ignore or avoid all this gossip? Yes, if you take a moment to think before you speak. Try responding to a juicy tidbit in one or more of the following ways:

1. "I'm sorry, I've been asked not to say anything."

2. "I'd rather not talk about it unless the people are here to defend themselves."

3. "I know I'd feel terrible if I knew people were talking about me this way."

4. "Maybe there are two sides to this and we don't know the whole story yet, so I'm not comfortable drawing any conclusions."

5. "You know, everyone makes mistakes—maybe we shouldn't be so quick to judge here."

6. "I promised to keep this confidential."

Even when you aren't best friends with the person you're protecting, you will reap positive benefits by refusing to gossip. You will gain a reputation as someone who:

- can be trusted
- keeps a secret
- is a loyal friend
- has integrity.

Not such a bad claim to fame, eh?

LIVE IT OUT!

This week, make a point of being the *opposite* of a gossip. Instead, be a confidential listener—one who respects and protects the secrets of another by keeping them *completely* to yourself.

Excel 'til the Bell

Some people love to strive for good grades as much as others love to play football. But for most of us, it's not easy to go above and beyond what we know we can do! So here's something to motivate you to go out and do your best.

"Never give up. Never give up. Never give up." (Winston Churchill)

"Winners work at things that the majority of people are not willing to do." (Dennis Waitley)

"He who has begun his task has half done it." (Horace)

"Procrastination is the thief of time." (Edward Young)

"Go the extra mile. Do more than you are asked to do!" (Dennis Waitley)

"Only two things stand between you and success—getting started and never quitting." (Robert H. Schuller)

● ● ● ● ●
LIVE IT OUT!

1. Is there one unfinished project or task that you've been putting off? _____

2. What are three things you can do to get started or to finish it?
    (a) _____
    (b) _____
    (c) _____

3. Robert Schuller has asked the question, "If you could attempt anything and not fail, what would it be?" Give *your* answer. _____

_____

4. What school subject do you most frequently put off doing?

_____

    (*Note:* Authorities on time management suggest that you should always tackle the most difficult or most boring project first to get it out of the way.)

5. Read Psalm 90:12 and rewrite it as your prayer today:

_____

_____

Handle with Accuracy

Because I travel a lot, I've often seen famous people—such as Goldie Hawn and Billie Jean King—in airports and hotels. Last fall, I had just checked into the Marriott Hotel in San Francisco. As I stumbled onto the elevator with all my luggage, I realized I couldn't find my room key; in fact, I didn't even know what floor to get off on! At that moment, I looked up at the other two people in the elevator: Joe Montana and his bodyguard! I nearly fell over!

I opened my mouth to say hello—and, in true Becky style, I forgot his name! But no way would I miss a chance to talk to good ol' What's-His-Name, so I grinned, shot out my right fist to punch his shoulder buddy-style, and said, "Hey, how ya doin'?" Then I immediately cracked up at myself for being such a nut! Fortunately, he cracked up too and said, "Just fine!"

Did I get his autograph? No! I was so taken aback by who he was that when he asked if he could help me with my luggage, I nonchalantly said "No thanks" and shuffled out of the elevator. I could have kicked myself afterwards! Well, I was so excited that for the next week, I told everyone I knew about riding the elevator with Joe Montana. (And did the 49ers win the Super Bowl that year? Yes!)

Everyone knows that Joe Montana is an incredible quarterback. He throws the ball with extreme accuracy and confidence. And he has endured and persevered to become one of the greatest quarterbacks of all time.

Have you ever considered handling the Bible with such accuracy that you became well known for it? In 2 Timothy 2:15 Paul writes, "Do your best to present yourself to God as one approved, a workman who does not need to be ashamed and who correctly handles the word of truth." Have you thought about the impact you could make in your high school if you were to lead a Bible study or begin a prayer meeting?

I've met a number of students who, against the odds—and sometimes even against the administration—have started a Christian group on their public high school campus. It wasn't easy, and some of them had to sacrifice activities they might have pursued if they weren't Christian leaders on their campus. Some were athletes, some played in the band, and some belonged to the honor society, but their desire to reach their school for Christ motivated them to study the Bible with other students and risk being known as Christians. Could God be calling you to do the same?

• • • • •
LIVE IT OUT!

Does your school have a Christian fellowship, a campus Bible study, or a prayer meeting? If so, do you attend? Why or why not?

_____

If your school does not currently have such a group, consider starting one. First, contact a Christian teacher or counselor at your school and find out when and where you could hold a meeting (thirty minutes before school starts, during lunch hour, immediately following the school day, etc.). Then, spread the word among your Christian (and even non-Christian!) friends.

If you are at all inspired to be a "workman" on your campus, brainstorm a few ideas for a group now and list people who might want to be involved:

_____

_____

_____

As you consider this possibility, ask yourself: How well do I handle (read, understand, share, and apply) the Word of God when I am with a friend or in a small group? What steps can I take to improve my accuracy? _____

_____

Leaving
Your Mark

I can't ever remember meeting a real Christian in high school. If I had, I think I would have remembered that . . .

- they acted different,
- they went to churchy events,
- they tried to get me to go (!)
- they didn't cuss,
- they had strong values and morals,
- they prayed and read a Bible,
- they felt uncomfortable with certain music or movies,
- they talked about God a lot, and they even wanted me to ask him into my heart.

I can't ever remember meeting—or knowing—any Christians in high school. I wish I had. Maybe I would have given them a hard time. Maybe I would have laughed at them. Or maybe I would have confided in them, noticed their inner strength, or respected their values. Maybe, just maybe, they could have shown me the way out of the party scene.

Maybe . . . if I had only met one.

• • • •
LIVE IT OUT!

Do people at your school know that you *know* Jesus? Do you have a reputation for being a Christian? Many students are afraid, embarrassed, or even unsure how to share their faith in school. Take a look at these Scriptures and ask yourself how you practice them in your daily life.

Romans 1:16 _____

1 Timothy 4:16 _____

Ephesians 5:8–11 _____

John 13:34–35 _____

1 Timothy 4:12 _____

What kind of mark are you leaving for Jesus in your school? _____

_____

Tomorrow, who is one person you could share with? _____

Peer Pressure

According to the Campus Life book *What Teenagers Are Saying about Drugs and Alcohol,* peer pressure is overwhelmingly the number-one reason that students drink in high school! If peer pressure is that powerful, how can a person beat it? Next time you feel the pressure coming to do something that compromises your beliefs or your good sense, try one or more of the following options:

P*ropose an alternative.* When you suggest a better idea (i.e. one that is moral or legal or safer), you will probably discover at least one other person in the group who feels as you do, but is too intimidated to say anything *unless* someone else does! You might even find that your idea becomes the "moral majority"!

E*xpress your feelings, reservations, and fears honestly.* Possibly the others will totally overlook and override your suggestions, but you owe it to yourself and to them to say how you are feeling and why.

Take the scenario of riding in a car in which the driver has been drinking. Are you uncomfortable? Are you afraid? Are you concerned about getting in trouble with the law? Say something. Sure, you risk sounding prudish or pious, but you may very well save a license—or a life!

E*scape whenever necessary.* Remember the promise of 1 Corinthians 10:13: "God is faithful; he will not let you be tempted beyond what you can bear. But when you are tempted, he will also provide a way out so that you can stand up under it." In high school there *will* be situations in which your only option is to bail out—to not join in, to leave the scene, to avoid any part of something that looks fun and may be popular, but is dead wrong. Look for God's escape—and take it!

Resist the devil. James 4:7 says, "Submit yourselves, then, to God. Resist the devil, and he will flee from you." Today, it is no secret that some students get into devil worship, ouija boards, tarot cards, witchcraft and horoscopes. On a recent trip, I met a guy who told me how he "fell" into the whole scene—and barely made it out. This is nothing to mess with. The word here is *resist*. Resist. Resist. Resist.

• • • • •
LIVE IT OUT!

Can you think of a recent time that you were in a compromising situation and you either should have proposed or did propose an alternative? Describe: _____

_____

What one group of people do you find it especially difficult to express your honest feelings to? Why? _____

_____

Think back to a previous time of temptation in which God provided an escape for you, but you didn't take it. In retrospect, how or why did you miss your escape? And how can you avoid the same mistake next time? _____

_____

_____

Read James 4 and underline or highlight verses that are particularly helpful to you in the area of resisting peer pressure.

Stand Up!

Abortion versus pro-choice. Creation versus evolution. Abstinence versus safe sex. How do you take a stand for what you believe is right in a public high school—especially when your teacher has a different set of values than you do?

Candy was raised by parents who not only had strong Christian beliefs, but who worked in Christian ministry. By the time she started college, she had developed a clear set of values and beliefs of her own. For instance, she not only knew that the Bible taught abstinence from premarital sex, but she personally chose to live by that teaching as well.

After only a few weeks on campus, she realized that people definitely considered her viewpoint to be old-fashioned and prudish. The comments, discussions, and lifestyles on campus never seemed to provide her a chance to share what she believed about this issue and why.

But then one day in her speech class she saw a great opportunity to talk about her faith and how it affected her lifestyle. Each student was asked to take a position on a topic and then defend it before the entire class a week later.

Candy did her homework—interviewing various people, researching statistics—and then presented her viewpoint to a very captive audience! Though the full impact of her speech on others may never be known, Candy knew that she had taken a stand for what she believed—with confidence and conviction!

• • • • •
LIVE IT OUT!

1 Timothy 4:12 says, "Don't let anyone look down on you because you are young, but set an example for the believers in speech, in life, in love, in faith and in purity." Think of an opportunity you might have, now or in the near future, to take a stand for something you believe in or feel strongly about.

What's the situation? _____

_____

What stand would you take? Why do you feel so strongly about this? _____

_____

_____

_____

_____

What impact might your stand have on those around you? _____

_____

What are a few ways that you might become an example to others at school in your . . .

speech: _____

life: _____

love: _____

faith: _____

purity: _____

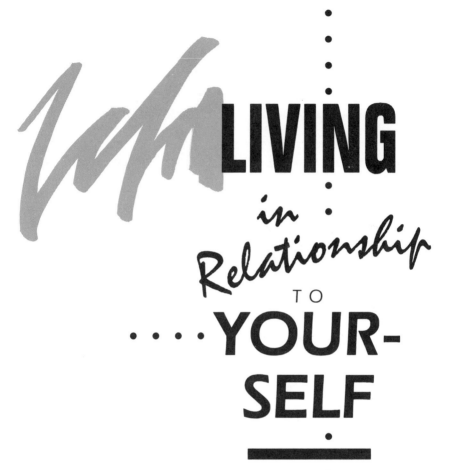

LIVING *in* *Relationship* TO YOUR-SELF

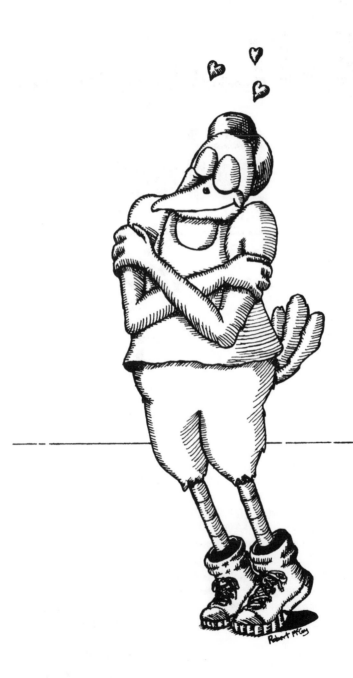

LIVE IT! and Like Yourself

Psychologists Say ...

Psychologists tell us that the number-one factor influencing our self-esteem is the person closest to us, such as a parent, a friend, or a sibling. In other words, how we think that person feels about us determines how *we* feel about ourselves. Now if that is true, then most of us are in trouble!

Though some are more fortunate than others, many of us have come from family backgrounds ranging from mediocre to lousy.

For example, thousands of students come from broken homes with only one parent. Others live in "blended" families with a stepparent—a stressful situation that can be filled with misunderstandings, arguments, high expectations, even abuse. Some live with parents who have been physically, sexually, or emotionally abusive because of alcohol or drug addiction or some other problem. If *these* are the people closest to us, then huge numbers of students must be feeling pretty terrible about themselves.

You know what? I meet those kinds of students all the time! The more I travel, the more I meet students who desperately need outside help in liking themselves—all because of the negative relationships they have with the people closest to them.

What do they look like? Oh, they often appear to be normal by the way they dress and dance and laugh, but if they spend any amount of time talking about life, I hear about their confused and damaged identity. They don't like themselves, believe in themselves, or respect themselves—again, because they weren't given the love and affirmation they needed from their families.

How do they act? That's where the problems surface. They are often promiscuous, and sometimes rude and disrespectful of authority. Others, especially young men, may be confused about their sexual identity. And lately I have met kids who have gotten involved in gangs, even Satanism, because people already involved in those groups offer them love, acceptance, and power that no one else has genuinely offered. Then there are lots of students who drink and use drugs because of the closeness, popularity, camaraderie, and attention they feel they're getting (and haven't gotten elsewhere)—even though it means doing things that they know are not right.

● ● ● ● ●

LIVE IT OUT!

This week, I'd like you to take a good, long, serious look at who you are, where you came from, and where you are going. Do you truly like yourself? Do you feel that the people closest to you—your parents, siblings, or best friends—are making it easier or harder for you to like yourself?

Then, I'd like you to genuinely consider where God fits into your life. Today, read—slowly—Psalm 139. Underline or highlight any verses that sound new to you about how well God knows you!

Confused

Recently I read the personal story of a young man who had fallen into a homosexual lifestyle. It began when he was just a child. First, a relative committed suicide. Then, an older kid molested him. By the time he was a teenager, he became confused about his identity. Because he had been raised in a Christian home, he felt very afraid and ashamed to tell anyone—especially his parents or youth pastor—about his struggle. He worried that they'd judge him.

So instead, he remained confused about his sexual identity and proceeded to spend the next few years of his life in a homosexual lifestyle, full of guilt, lying, hiding, sin and shame. Eventually, just before he died of AIDS, he told his story to help others see the importance of *getting help* when you are confused about who you are.

When you worry that no one loves you, or that you're not worth loving, or you question who you are and what you were meant to be (sexually or otherwise) and why you feel the way you do, that is the time to talk to someone who can help you.

If you are one of the very special people I've just described, and you feel low and lousy about yourself, I want to assure you that you have a God who loves you. If you feel inadequate, insecure, afraid, embarrassed, ashamed, suicidal, or lost, I want to encourage you today that there is help for you. But you *must* tell someone you need help. Now. Not later. Not after it's too late.

• • • • •
LIVE IT OUT!

If you *are* confused about your identity or need to talk to someone—about anything—please start by sharing with someone such as a pastor, older friend, parent, or school counselor. Yes, it will be difficult and painful to talk about such a deeply personal issue. But waiting until more time has passed can be much more harmful.

If you can't confide in anyone you know right now, then consider calling a service such as the National Youth Crisis Hotline. By dialing 1-800-HIT-HOME, you can talk anonymously and confidentially with a caring counselor. But whoever you decide to talk to, please do it now.

The S.E.L.F. Test

Orphans. Adoptees. Victims of abuse or abandonment. Rich kids. Poor kids. Valedictorians. Beauty queens. Student Council presidents. Quarterbacks. Studs. Athletic types. Artists. Nerds.

Don't be fooled: *everyone* struggles with self-image!

So what does it take for a student to have a healthy self-image? How can you know who you are and feel good about yourself?

Over the next four days, I'd like you to take a S.E.L.F. test to help you to see how healthy your self-image is. There will be a specific question for each day:

S Is your *security* in God?
E Do you *evaluate* yourself often?
L Do you *love* yourself?
F How do you *feel* about yourself?

• • • • •
LIVE IT OUT!

Before you get into the S.E.L.F. test, check out these four specific things the Bible says about your self-image:

1. God evaluates a person's worth differently than humans do (James 2:1–7; Luke 16:15).

2. God says he made us perfectly (Psalm 139:13–16).

3. God loves us no matter what (Romans 8:31–39).

4. Because God loves us, we can love others (1 John 4:7–11).

Security in God

It's sad but true: often our parents, brothers, sisters, friends, coaches, teachers, and employers can be our greatest source of

disapproval,
disappointment,
demeaning remarks,
discouragement,
devastation, and
disruption.

If we can't find our security in these people, then who *can* we trust? Only God loves every person unconditionally. Only God loved the people of the world so much (even though they didn't love him!) that he gave up his son to die for them. Only God has the character to forgive—and forget—the sins of imperfect people! Only God created us with a specific plan for our lives. Only God can take a broken life and turn it into something beautiful. Not only *can* we get our security from God, we *must!*

● ● ● ● ●
LIVE IT OUT!

Look up the following Scriptures:

Romans 3:23; 5:8; 6:23; 10:9–10. Ask yourself, "How much does God love me? Do I know anyone else who loves me that much?"

Psalm 139:13–16 talks about your creation. What in this passage sounds new to you? What do you like about its message?

Psalm 138:8 says that the Lord *will* fulfill his purpose for you. Did you know you have a purpose? What do you think it might be?

Evaluate Often

In junior high I was a total jock. I was captain of the cheerleaders, and I was on the field hockey, basketball, and synchronized swim teams. I loved sports—and was always happier when I was active than when I was sitting still.

When I entered high school, I got the impression that girls who were jocks were not as attractive or as popular as the girls who were cheerleaders. So within a few weeks, I quit the swim team I had competed with since sixth grade, and dropped out of every sport except for cheerleading. I wanted to be popular. Little did I know that I was giving up not only what made me happy, but what truly made me who I was!

With all my extra time and much less activity, two significant changes took place. First, I gained weight, and second, I had to find new friends because I was no longer hanging out with my usual teammates at sports practices.

Both of those changes had a real effect on my self-image. I was no longer trying to be myself; instead, I was trying to be and act like the kind of person I thought *others* wanted me to be. I started to hang out with older students who had a lot of time after school and didn't work. We would go out cruising—smoking and drinking and later doing drugs. My appearance changed, my style of clothes changed (for the worse), and my motivation for doing anything slipped to zero.

My dream of being a physical education teacher and high school coach died when I gave up sports in the tenth grade. And my dream of being the varsity cheerleading captain fizzled out, too: I never even bothered to try out for varsity cheerleading in my last year of high school—even though I had dreamed about it since I was in first grade.

I left those dreams behind when I neglected to be who I was meant to be because it didn't seem cool enough or popular enough. But in the end, who lost out? My friends? No, they didn't lose a thing.

I was the one who lost out.

• • • • •

LIVE IT OUT!

The **E** in the S.E.L.F. test is for *evaluate*. Evaluate yourself often. Every time you enter a new school, begin a new school year, or consider dropping an activity you've been involved in for a long time, do yourself a big favor and ask:

Am I really acting or being like the person I know I am?

Am I prematurely giving up on a dream out of fear or discouragement, or am I doing this to pursue a different dream?

If I change friends, will it ultimately help me or hurt me as a person?

Am I doing what *I* want to do, or am I doing this because of what *someone else* thinks or wants? Am I afraid of being rejected if I don't do this?

Can I trust God to provide friends who won't reject me if I do (or don't do) this?

Now, read Philippians 2:3 and 1:6, and paraphrase them in your own words.

Love Yourself

The third part of the S.E.L.F. test is to *love yourself!* This can be difficult, uncomfortable, and even destructive if it is based on an egotistical, self-centered conceit. But in Matthew 19:19, Jesus said, "Love your neighbor as yourself." What did he mean?

Look at it this way. When you love other people, you treat them with respect, kindness, consideration, dignity, and care. You love them because they are important to you—they are valuable in your eyes.

The same is true for ourselves. Each one of us—no matter who we are, where we live, how much we have, or who we are related to—is infinitely valuable to God! He loves each and every one of us in a personal way. And if we are so special and valuable to God, then it makes sense to love ourselves (i.e., treat ourselves with kindness, respect, care, and dignity) just as much as we love others.

Denis Waitley, a speaker who motivates people to do great things, often starts his talks by saying, "We must feel love inside before we can give it away." If you are constantly saying things like, "I hate myself. I wish I could die. Nobody loves me," then it's time to take a huge step and look at your life as God sees it—so infinitely valuable to him that he would give his own Son's life for you (John 3:16).

When you begin to *believe* that you are very valuable to God, and that he loves you *so much*, you will find it so much easier to love others.

Why should we base our self-esteem on how much *God* loves us? Because the love of other people is often "conditional" (qualified with ifs and buts). God's love, on the other hand, *never* changes. He will never leave us or forsake us (Deuteronomy 31:8). Take a minute now to think quietly about how much God loves you today. Then go out and give some of that love away!

● ● ● ● ●
LIVE IT OUT!

Can you honestly say that you love yourself? _____

Do you find it uncomfortable to say? _____

Read John 3:16 and insert your name in place of "the world."

Earl Palmer, a pastor from Berkeley, California, recently said, "You prove that you are loved when you are able to love someone else." On a scale of 1 to 10 (10 being high), how's your:

Love for yourself	1 2 3 4 5 6 7 8 9 10
Love for others	1 2 3 4 5 6 7 8 9 10

Feelings

The last part of the S.E.L.F. test is *feelings*. Feelings *are* an indicator of healthy—or unhealthy—self-esteem.

A friend of mine who has worked with high school students for almost twenty years feels strongly that the rise in homosexuality and promiscuity in students is directly related to inappropriate feelings about themselves.

When students have terrible home lives that cause them to doubt their own value, they will often cheapen themselves around others just to be accepted or loved. Sometimes physical characteristics such as height, weight, complexion, coordination, or whatever, can cause a student to feel totally worthless.

At this point in the S.E.L.F. test, I would like to give you a mega-dose of encouragement! If you have strong feelings of doubt or confusion, or extremely low self-esteem, *please* give yourself permission to talk with someone about them, even if it feels scary to do so. I know too many people who have held these feelings inside and suffered greatly as a result.

What do I mean? When you hide these feelings, rather than get them out into the open and discuss them with someone who can help you understand them, they can grow inside of you like cancer. Jealousy, anger, even confused sexual identity can get bigger and bigger and become destructive if you don't share them with a trained counselor or youth worker.

It's a fact of life: *Everyone* needs someone to talk to.

I remember feeling very angry and confused about my home life, and the rejection I felt when my dad never attended my sports events. I remember how jealous I was of girls who had nicer clothes and homes and cars. I avoided talking about those feelings with a counselor or pastor, or even with my older brother or sister, because I was embarrassed. Instead, I became an "escape artist." I drank, partied, shoplifted, and became promiscuous—all in order to deal with my feelings of inadequacy. I fell into a six-year pattern of personal problems—from age fifteen to twenty-one—and I'm still carrying some of those scars with me today.

Honestly, if I could do those years over again, I would. I can even think of people who were there and could have helped me— if I had only opened up to them. If I can encourage you now to take a chance and talk to someone—a teacher, a guidance counselor, a pastor, a youth sponsor, or volunteer—I *know* it can make a difference in who you are and where you are going! Do it, okay?

• • • • •
LIVE IT OUT!

What are some of the inner feelings about yourself that you struggle with regularly? _____

_____

Who can you sit down with to talk with about these feelings?

_____

_____

Would you make an appointment to get together with that person in the next week? Remember, you've got everything to gain!

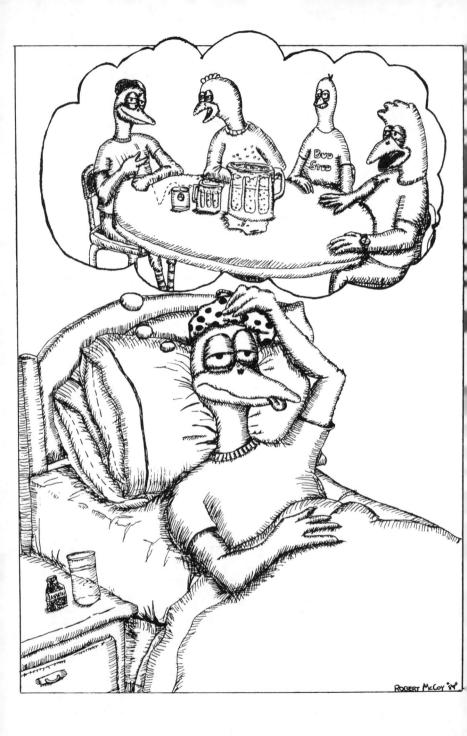

LIVE IT! *without Drugs and Alcohol*

Fallin' All Over the Place ...

When you drink, most of the time you want one of two things:

• to have fun, or
• to forget your troubles, i.e., escape.

Most kids who drink *don't* say, "Let's go get drunk so that I can

... make a fool of myself."
... get in a car accident."
... hurt myself or someone else."
... lose my driver's license."
... sleep around."

But if you are a student who regularly drinks, you've more than likely begun to establish some of those patterns.

Or possibly:

You *can't remember* some of the things you did while you were drinking recently.

You *are ashamed* or even humiliated about some of the things you said or did while drinking.

You've *gotten into trouble* (after drinking) with someone in authority because of a smart mouth, inability to drive safely, or loss of temper.

You have *the ability to consume much more alcohol* than most everyone else.

How do I know these things happen to students who drink? Well, let's just say that it takes one to know one. I'm certainly not proud of the fact that I was a teenage alcoholic, but as a student who drank regularly, I didn't know that my symptoms (some of which are listed above) were signs of alcoholism. At that time, I thought alcoholics were people who drank alone, drank in the morning, or couldn't hold their liquor.

From the ages of fifteen to twenty-one, I progressed through many stages of alcoholism without ever knowing, believing, or admitting that I was an alcoholic. That's why, when I speak to students, I tell them my story—and the *incredible* dangers involved in drinking—so they might be able to see that their "fun" escapades could be turning into a serious drinking problem or even alcoholism.

Almost every time I speak, someone confides in me that they might have a drinking problem, and many tell me that their parents are alcoholics. If you and I had the chance to sit and talk about the temptation to drink, my greatest words of advice (gained from learning the hard way) would be: Consider the consequences *before* you say yes. It's a decision that could affect—if not ruin—your entire life.

• • • • •

LIVE IT OUT!

Take this short true/false quiz on your knowledge of alcohol and its effects:

	TRUE	FALSE
1. Alcohol is a drug.	☐	☐
2. Alcoholics are people who cannot control their drinking.	☐	☐
3. Alcohol lowers the inhibitions of the drinker.	☐	☐

	TRUE	FALSE
4. Children of alcoholics are born with the tendency to become alcoholics.	☐	☐
5. You cannot become an alcoholic on beer or wine.	☐	☐
6. The younger a person starts drinking, the faster alcoholism develops.	☐	☐
7. Alcoholics do not have a limiting mechanism within them to cue them to stop drinking.	☐	☐
8. Alcoholism is a disease.	☐	☐
9. Alcoholism can be outgrown (i.e., once an alcoholic has become sober, in time he can drink moderately).	☐	☐
10. Alcoholics can consume vast quantities of liquor.	☐	☐

Now check the answers and see how you did. More than anything, I want you to be fully aware of the facts about alcohol, today's drug of choice—especially if you are the child of an alcoholic.

1. *True.* Yes, it contains ethyl alcohol.

2. *False.* Not always—in the early stages it may appear that a person is controlling their alcohol, but in later stages they will not be able to control it.

3. *True.* Especially one's moral judgment; for example, socially or in dating relationships.

4. *True.* Research shows that children of alcoholics have a much higher risk of becoming alcoholics if they drink.

5. *False.* Alcohol is alcohol.

6. *True.* In fact, a student can progress through the stages of alcoholism in three years, where it might take an adult twenty years.

7. *True*. No, they are not born with a limiting mechanism, and therefore they can never be "social drinkers."

8. *True*. For years alcoholism was considered by many as mental illness, but it is a treatable disease.

9. *False*. An alcoholic can never drink moderately; it will eventually get out of control.

10. *True*. Yes, this is the common trait of all alcoholics.

The information for this quiz (and many more facts) comes from *Growing Up Addicted*, an excellent book by Steve Arterburn, founder of the New Life Treatment Centers. If you have any more questions about alcohol or drug abuse, I would encourage you to go to a library or bookstore and read for yourself. And if this quiz has brought up any fears about yourself or someone you know, make an appointment with someone you trust and talk about it.

Little Joe

Last winter I spoke at a ski retreat in Colorado. After sharing my story the first night, I offered to hang out in the main room to talk with anyone about drinking—or anything else. The last person I would ever have expected to show up was "Little Joe." At 250 lbs., he was the biggest, funniest, and rowdiest guy in the whole group of 250 kids! But when he peeked into the room with a shy, hesitant look, I knew something was up.

Finding me alone, he asked if we could talk privately. As it turned out, he was a big party boy. But tonight was the first time he had ever listened to someone share the warning signs of alcoholism—and they described him! He was scared. He wondered what it might mean to admit to himself and to others that he was an alcoholic and that he wanted to stop drinking. He might possibly have to change his friends, his language, and most definitely his weekend lifestyle. It almost seemed overwhelming.

Then I shared what I really believed was a first step that he needed to take. There would be many more steps to come, but he could begin this one right then:

"Little Joe," I said, "I think you need to admit to Jesus that you have a problem and that you need forgiveness for your past. Then ask him to come into your heart and to take over your life. After that, you'll have to take another big step of faith to trust him to walk you through the steps to recovery." I had given this exact same advice to other guys and had gotten various reactions, such as "I'm not ready to ask Jesus into my life," or "I don't think I really have that big of a problem," or "I just can't do it," so I wasn't sure how Little Joe would respond.

"Becky," he said, "I think I'm an alcoholic. And I'll never be able to change my lifestyle, my friends, or my drinking without Jesus. My friends may not dig this, especially because I'm kind of the leader in my group, but I want to ask Jesus into my life. I want to change. I want to quit drinking." So, without further discussion, we prayed.

The next night, Little Joe stood up and told the whole roomful of kids and staff what his life had been like (some of the youth leaders from his church were sure surprised), and that he thought he was an alcoholic. Then, choking through a few tears, he went on to say that he had just asked Jesus to come into his life and that he knew God would help him to change! Mouths dropped open, some kids gasped and looked at each other in amazement, but everyone spontaneously broke into applause and cheers of support for his brave decision!

Five months later I got a letter from Little Joe. He was wondering if I could tell him how to get started talking to students about alcohol and its dangers. He also asked how he could help others invite Jesus into their lives and make them new, just as he had experienced!

• • • • •
LIVE IT OUT!

Little Joe is a great example of a student who faced his problem, admitted it to himself and others, and trusted Jesus with his life—problems and all! Maybe you have a friend who you think has a drinking problem, or maybe you struggle with drinking yourself. Here are a few things you can do first (adapted from the first three steps of the Twelve Step program):

1. Admit that you are powerless over certain areas of your life (such as drugs and/or alcohol).

2. Ask Jesus to come into your life.

3. Give Jesus control of your life by making a decision to turn your will and life over to him.

Today, if you are at a point in your life where you need to take these steps or make these decisions, take a minute to kneel beside your bed, if that is possible, and pray this prayer:

"Dear Lord, I cannot control this problem that I have in my life. I need you to come into my life. Lord Jesus, forgive me of my sins, and take control of my life and my will. I need your help. Please, Lord, I give you my life—problems and all. Help me. In Jesus' name I pray, Amen."

Read these Scriptures for further help: Romans 7:18; Philippians 2:13; Romans 12:1–2; 2 Corinthians 5:17; and 1 John 1:9. In addition, if you need to talk to someone right away, please call 1-800-332-TEEN.

Be Filled

Recently I was on a radio show with my friend Steve Arterburn of the New Life Treatment Centers. In the middle of the interview, he said something I had never heard before, but that really made a lot of sense.

He said that another word for alcohol is *spirits*, because the user attained the same kind of excitement, euphoria, and escape that is attached to a spiritual experience. In other words, when people drink, they are really looking to find comfort, escape, relief, excitement, and fun in much the same way some people experience God. But unfortunately, they are trying to fill their need for God with a counterfeit! Steve went on to explain that a person who tries to get power from alcohol limits his ability to get power from God. "Have you ever met an active alcoholic who has a great relationship with God?" he said. It's impossible, because you can't have a good relationship with both at the same time!

As a former alcoholic, I can really relate to the idea of looking for a "high" every time I drank. I never once drank because it tasted good. Nor did I ever have just one! Alcohol always provided me with an experience, but the longer I drank, the less comforting and exciting the experiences became. And I always needed more liquor to get a better high.

Ephesians 5:18 makes it clear that alcohol should not be substituted for experiencing God: "Do not get drunk on wine, which leads to debauchery [boozing]. Instead, be filled with the Spirit." How does this verse fit in to your lifestyle?

• • • • •

LIVE IT OUT!

The following verses talk about the lifestyle and consequences of the "drunkard": Proverbs 23:19–21; Proverbs 20:1; Romans 13:13; 1 Corinthians 6:10; and 1 Peter 4:3. Take a look at these and write a few sentences below on how God views drinking, drunkenness, and its consequences.

Your Future...
Today,
Tomorrow, and
Forever

The Twelve Step program is a series of steps that were developed originally for alcoholics, but now have been used successfully to help people face many kinds of problems: overeating, drug abuse, gambling, and more. They guide a person through specific actions or attitudes that they can take in order to find healing and freedom from their addiction—one day at a time.

Perhaps there are two kinds of students reading this today. Some of you may have gone through a treatment program or are involved in a support group for alcohol or drug abusers. Others of you haven't experienced addiction before and may not understand how important these twelve steps are to a parent or friend who is attending such a group.

If you are the first kind of student, I'd like to say: Don't stop being a part of a group where you are getting help! Often, students in recovery from an addiction do well for a time, but then they break away from their support system and find themselves slipping back into their habit. At that critical point when they need help most, they feel too ashamed to go back, admit they've messed up, and submit to the necessary help and advice to get back on track.

Please don't ever give up your battle to be free of your addiction. We are all different and will recover in different ways. Though some people may find healing more quickly than others, most need to continue in treatment, group therapy, or sponsorship for months and possibly years—until they have developed the inner strength to resist the habit. Don't ever stop fighting to win over your addiction. You may lose a little ground and a lot of pride at times, but if you don't give up, in the end you will gain a future of happiness by attacking your addiction until it is overcome!

Are you the second kind of student I described? Then this is your opportunity to be a great friend or an understanding son or daughter (if you have an alcoholic parent). Do all that you can to be sensitive, encouraging, and well-informed about your friend's or parent's addiction. As he or she continues to work through a Twelve Step program, you can serve as a confidential support person. Remember, *support* their recovery program. Gossip or ridicule can inflict unnecessary embarrassment or guilt on someone trying to break free from his addiction.

• • • • •
LIVE IT OUT!

If you are an addictive/compulsive person: What is your most recent concern or struggle? Have you asked someone to help? If not, who could you pick up the phone and call right now?

_____

Review the Twelve Steps listed on the next page and identify where you are at this point. _____

_____

If you are the friend, son, or daughter of an addictive/compulsive person: Have you ever offered to go with him or her to a support group? Why or why not? What's keeping you from offering (or offering again) right now? _____

_____

From looking at the Twelve Steps, what do you learn about the process an alcoholic (or addict) must go through in order to change? _____

_____

Now run through the list again, substituting the word "problem" for "alcohol" and "others" for "alcoholics." (Try getting even more specific by plugging in an *actual* problem you're facing for the word "alcohol.") What help or insight might the Twelve Steps be giving you? _____

_____

The Twelve Steps

1. We admitted we were powerless over alcohol—that our lives had become unmanageable.

2. Came to believe that a Power greater than ourselves could restore us to sanity.

3. Made a decision to turn our will and our lives over to the care of God *as we understood Him.*

4. Made a searching and fearless moral inventory of ourselves.

5. Admitted to God, to ourselves, and to another human being the exact nature of our wrongs.

6. Were entirely ready to have God remove all these defects of character.

7. Humbly asked Him to remove our shortcomings.

8. Made a list of all persons we had harmed, and became willing to make amends to them all.

9. Made direct amends to people wherever possible, except when to do so would injure them or others.

10. Continued to take personal inventory and when we were wrong promptly admitted it.

11. Sought through prayer and meditation to improve our conscious contact with God *as we understood Him,* praying only for knowledge of His will for us and the power to carry that out.

12. Having had a spiritual awakening as the result of these Steps, we tried to carry this message to others, and to practice these principles in all our affairs.[1]

Friends Won't Let You Down...

. . . or will they? After my first three months of sobriety, I went out with my old group of buddies. I was really excited to tell them about all of the changes I had made in my life! I thought they'd be just as excited for me as I was, but I was wrong. They couldn't seem to handle it when I described myself and my problem by saying, "I'm an alcoholic." They would say, "Becky, you aren't an alcoholic. You just need to slow down a little." I knew better, but since I wasn't yet able to deal with any major rejection, I mellowed with the "alcoholic" jargon and tried to be my old self.

But the next time we got together, we did what we always did—we went drinking. And I slipped—hard. I had tried to control my drinking that night, but when I got dropped off at home, I proceeded to polish off a half gallon of wine that I knew was stashed under the sink. My first and last drinking night with my old buddies ended with me passed out on my parents' kitchen floor.

Lying in my bed the next morning, hung over and humiliated, I realized that if I was ever going to stay sober, (1) I could not go out with my old friends, and (2) I could never have "just one drink." I had to stop completely.

After that night—more than thirteen years ago—it turned out that I never, ever went out with those friends again. Though at times I felt rejected, betrayed, disappointed, and lonely, God

---
[1]*Alcoholics Anonymous* (New York: Alcoholics Anonymous Publishing, Inc., 1981).

allowed me to get involved with a whole new group of Christian friends. Eventually I got into youth ministry, met my husband—and with God's help, I've been sober ever since!

• • • •

LIVE IT OUT!

If you haven't heard it already, at some point in your life you may hear people tell you that the friends you're hanging out with aren't doing you any good. They may suggest that you need to change friends or give up some of them—especially the ones that you aren't strong enough to hang out with. If someone ever says these things to you (even if they don't say it very compassionately), do yourself a favor: *Listen.* I wish I had.

As you read this, if you get a twinge or feeling that you are hanging out with some people that you know aren't good for you, *do what you need to do to make a change.* Take a few minutes to think about your life, and then pray for the strength and the guts to make some changes. You gotta do it. You gotta do it.

Read Ephesians 4:22–25 for some good advice.

Family Ties

I knew where they kept the whiskey. I knew where the beer was. And I knew how to drink my parents' liquor and make it look as if I hadn't had any. I even shared their booze with my friends! For years, my parents never knew how much or how often I drank from their liquor supply.

One winter night, to save money, my boyfriend and another couple came over to my house. My parents rarely went out, but on this night they had gone to a wedding. So I thought I'd take advantage of a good thing and have a private party.

Since we didn't know exactly how long my parents would be

gone, we drank shots of whiskey from the kitchen cupboard and washed them down with beer to get a quicker buzz. (It worked.) By 9:00 P.M., my boyfriend and I had staggered over to the living room couch, more loaded than passionate.

When I heard the front door creak a while later, I only had enough time to lift my head and see my dad's silhouette in the doorway. He had no clue that I was home . . . yet. But as soon as the lights went on, the shouting started and I was in big trouble. That night was one of the first times that I ran away from home.

Getting drunk had become a part of my lifestyle by then. I didn't care that it bothered my parents; in fact, I was angry at them for interrupting my party. I had become rebellious and deceptive when it came to drinking, even risking getting caught in my own home with my parents' liquor. I wish someone would have told me then that I had a problem.

• • • • •

LIVE IT OUT!

Check out these two Scriptures in order to understand what the Bible says about drunkenness. Write down the main point of each passage.

2 Timothy 2:22 _____

1 Thessalonians 5:4–8 _____

I know you don't need anyone to tell you that drinking your parents' liquor is not wise, but if you need someone to give you a kick in the pants to stop, consider this a kick.

Forgiven—a Reason for Livin'!

As an alcoholic who had done so many hurtful things to so many people, I knew that my parents, my boyfriend, my boss, and others wouldn't be quick to forgive me when I decided to change. One of the things that most contributed to my healing—and sped up my recovery process—was to realize that if I confessed my sins to God, *he* would be faithful to forgive me (1 John 1:9). When I took time to do this, I experienced feelings of relief, joy, freedom, and hope! I felt clean!

When Ralph, a church janitor, led me to the Lord on August 26, 1976, I experienced a spontaneous healing from the *desire* to drink (though I could become addicted again if I ever took another drink). When I prayed and asked Christ into my life, Ralph told me that according to 2 Corinthians 5:17, I had become a brand new person! He said that the old things of my life would pass away and that all things would become new. No other person or thing had that kind of power to change me. Only Jesus.

I really attribute much of my dramatic conversion and healing to Ralph's confidence in the Word of God. The next miracle was that I believed him: I was forgiven and new! From that moment on, I proceeded to experience *radical* changes in every area of my life.

• • • •
LIVE IT OUT!

If today's reading gives you a ray of hope for healing, hang on to it. And let these words soak in, too:

"Do not worry about tomorrow, for tomorrow will worry about itself. Each day has enough trouble of its own" (Matthew 6:34). *Take it one day at a time!*

"Do not be anxious about anything, but in everything . . . present your requests to God" (Philippians 4:6). *Pray at all times!*

Confess and be cleansed (1 John 1:9).

Become new! (2 Corinthians 5:17).

Whether you're suffering from an addiction or from some other problem, is this your day for a fresh start? Just open your heart. Give your life to God. Let him in!

ROBERT McCOY '89

Everything— for Nothing!

"More Go All the Way," the eye-catching headline read in a special issue of *Newsweek* (Summer/Fall 1990). The headline didn't surprise me, but the statistics that followed sure did:

Percentage of Girls Having Sex

Age	1979	1988
15	22%	27%
17	47%	52%
19	65%	78%

Percentage of Guys Having Sex

Age	1979	1988
15	NA	33%
17	56%	66%
19	78%	86%

In the *Newsweek* article, which was entitled "A Much Riskier Passage," students from around the country vividly and unashamedly chronicled their sexual exploits and escapades. In addition, the article quoted a poll that suggests most teens are regularly having sexual intercourse by the eleventh grade. And what's more, the article said that about 500,000 teenage girls give birth every year!

Those are the statistics. And believe it or not, all that I've read or heard suggests *Christian students are only five percent less sexually active than non-Christians!* Why is this so? There are plenty of reasons, such as

- poor self-image,
- fear of rejection,
- ignorance about God's Word,
- a longing for love, or
- the need for a father image.

If the statistics are any indication, sex outside of marriage doesn't seem to be slowing down! Musician Tim Miner is certainly aware of this, and presents a powerful perspective on casual sex in the following song:

> Why you wanna walk and talk a lie
> Why you wanna kiss your life good-bye
> Why you wanna risk everything
> For the pleasure one moment brings?
>
> Everybody wants to get ahead
> Everybody says you go to bed
> Never knew how their tactics worked
> When they're wakin' up with a jerk
>
> So-called friends puttin' pressure on
> Can't you tell what's right, what's wrong?
> So you really think you've grown up wise
> Sixteen, hopin' you'll survive
> You're way too casual . . .
> *Way too casual.*[1]

---

[1]"Too Casual" by Tim Miner and Cindy Cruz. © 1988 Birdwing Music/Tim Miner Music/Rhettrhyme Publishing (Birdwing Music/Tim Miner Music division of Sparrow Corp., Box 5010, Brentwood, TN 37024). Rhettrhyme Music, BMG Songs, Inc. 1988-91. All rights reserved. International copyright secured. Used by permission.

LIVE IT OUT!

If you've ever been tempted to fall into the sex trap, can you remember *why* and *when* you weakened? These are *very* important patterns or moments to think about, because they could help you understand what is *really* going on in this area of your life.

Next, talk with a Christian counselor, pastor, mentor, or youth director and allow yourself to be accountable to them in this area! It might save you a *lot* of heartache, especially if you struggle frequently in this area. Please make an appointment today!

P.S. For more advice and Scripture on this subject, see the section entitled "Live It! . . . on Your Dates."

Parental Discretion Advised

The week before school started, Tom, a junior-high friend of mine, had a chance to go to Magic Mountain (a roller-coaster park) with Chad, an older friend. He had never been allowed to go to places like that alone before, but he talked over the whole thing with his parents. They were kind of strict about some things, such as the music he could listen to and the movies he could see, so allowing him to go to Magic Mountain alone would be a big step.

Tom was thrilled when his parents decided he could go—on one condition: that he would meet up with Chad's parents for dinner and then hang out with them for the rest of the evening.

As I remember the story, Chad's family's car pulled into the driveway at 1:00 A.M. When Tom's mom went outside to meet and greet them, they all seemed unusually quiet.

"So how'd it go?" she said. "Did you have fun?" It was dark outside, but she could hear in their tone of voice that something was wrong.

The minute Tom walked into the house, his mom looked at him and said, "Did something happen?" Tom couldn't hold it in for one minute. He sat down and spilled the whole story—how he told Chad's parents he *didn't* have to stick with them, how he then met up with some kids who did wild and risky things, and then how he began to say foolish things himself in order to fit in!

And it had all happened in one night! So many things Tom had *never* expected to say or see or do had all occurred in a few short hours. He had never experienced such peer pressure before.

But in talking to his mom, Tom realized something: All of those "things" (which he truly felt ashamed of and sorry for) had happened *immediately after* he broke the one non-negotiable rule he had set up with his parents—sticking with Chad's parents for the evening.

That night Tom learned a major lesson about the safety and security in obeying a parent's advice. What initially appeared to be a strict rule would have spared him a slew of messy consequences if he had obeyed it!

• • • • •
LIVE IT OUT!

Think of a time when you disobeyed your parents' advice. Apart from any punishment you received, what negative consequences could you have avoided? _____

_____

Is there a parental rule you are currently disobeying secretly and know you should stop (such as seeing a boyfriend or girlfriend you've been asked not to see, hanging out somewhere you've been forbidden to go, etc.)? Look up the Scriptures listed below, and then honestly ask yourself: What adjustments do I need to make in my respect for or obedience to my parents?

Deuteronomy 6:1–2 _____

Ephesians 6:1–3 _____

Colossians 3:20 _____

Deuteronomy 32:44–47 _____

Do the Right Thing

Jim, a strong Christian, was playing summer college baseball in Humboldt, California. One hot day when the team wasn't playing, he and a few teammates took off for some white-water rafting. Jim didn't know the other guys very well, as it was near the beginning of the season, but he looked forward to a good time.

On the way, they decided to stop for something cold to drink. The driver pulled into a back-country liquor store, and all six hot, thirsty guys piled out of the truck. Inside, Jim headed for the Coke cooler. Four of the others grabbed a six-pack of beer.

The fifth guy, apparently surprised that a teammate didn't drink on his day off, looked at Jim and asked, "Are you getting *Coke*?"

The question didn't bother Jim. He simply answered, "Yeah, just Coke—I don't drink beer."

"Oh," the guy replied. "Well, I guess I'll get Coke, too—I don't really feel like drinking."

When the other four guys, six-packs in hand, noticed the two Coke drinkers, they looked surprised. But then they shrugged their shoulders, put the beer back, and grabbed their own six-packs of Coke!

Not one word was spoken to convince those guys to skip the beer. Jim simply "did the right thing." And his action served to motivate the others to do the right thing, too!

• • • • •
LIVE IT OUT!

Did you ever imagine that "doing the right thing" might be exactly the kind of leadership people are looking for? You might not believe it until you try it. So, this week, at your first opportunity to act on what you believe is right, take a risk and *do* what is right. Watch what happens. Then turn back to this page and record the results.

_____

_____

_____

_____

For further encouragement, read 2 Thessalonians 3:13; Ephesians 5:15–16; Galatians 6:1–5, 9.

Worth the Dare?

I remember heading for the mall one Friday night with a bunch of friends—our typical weekend activity. But this night felt a little more intense, because we planned to do some serious shoplifting. We had done it plenty of times before, but had only taken small stuff—make-up, inexpensive jewelry, etc. Tonight would be different.

None of us were poor. And no one would have ever suspected us as thieves or vandals. There just seemed to be some curious adventure to the whole idea of shoplifting. So on this evening, we marched right up to the Juniors department of our favorite store.

Top Forty music blared from every corner amid pulsating colored lights, giving you the feeling of a dance floor. We tried on lots of clothes (leaving a few of them on underneath our own), bought one or two inexpensive pieces between the three of us, and nonchalantly left the mall.

There was no doubt in my mind that shoplifting was illegal. But someone had dared me to go for it. Even as I write this, I don't think my parents ever knew that I got into shoplifting. If I had been caught, they would have been humiliated, incredibly angry, and ashamed of me. In fact, I could never wear the dress I stole without having to sneak it out of the house or without feeling guilty. There was very little reward in my pickup other than not getting caught.

But a high school friend of mind did. She, unfortunately, was over eighteen years old and had to face felony charges in court. Worth the dare?

• • • • •
LIVE IT OUT!

Shoplifting *is* a harmful, habit-forming type of behavior. Perhaps you haven't shoplifted before, but you may have been tempted in the past or might be in the future.

If the situation ever arose, what would you say or do to discourage your friends from shoplifting? _____

_____

_____

What might be an appropriate Scripture passage or two that you could share with that person? _____

_____

_____

_____

If you have been involved in shoplifting and are finding it hard to stop, seek out a confidential person who can help you take the necessary steps to confront this problem. Do it now, before it's too late!

"Know When to Say When"?

I don't think I've ever seen a more outrageously ridiculous commercial than the one that *encourages* beer drinkers to "know when to say when"! Come on!

Would we have millions of alcoholics running around our country if people knew when they've had enough to drink? Or do you really think people would purposely drink, drive, and kill people (themselves *and* others) if they "knew when to say when"?

Steve Arterburn's book, *Growing Up Addicted*, reminds us that alcoholics are people who do *not* have a limiting mechanism in their system to tell them to stop drinking when (a) they've had too much, (b) they're intoxicated and shouldn't drive, or (c) they're not in control over their moral judgment any longer.

Someone who is progressing through the stages of alcoholism *doesn't* know when to say when! So don't fool yourself: If you've been having a problem with alcohol, don't tempt yourself by having one, or only a few. It just doesn't work!

In my opinion, *never drinking* is a much safer, happier option for students than trying to "control" your drinking, especially if you are a child of an alcoholic. Statistics and surveys tell us that nearly all students will be tempted to drink before they graduate from high school, and some even before they leave junior high. You owe it to yourself to know the facts about alcohol, alcohol abuse, and alcoholism.

• • • •
LIVE IT OUT!

If you have a problem with alcohol, know someone who does, or are just looking to be wise, get some good resources and information on the topic. You might even ask your youth director to have a meeting on drug and alcohol abuse.

Optional Reading:

Steve Arterburn, *Growing Up Addicted* (New York: Ballantine Books, 1989).
Becky Tirabassi, *Life of the Party* (Grand Rapids: Zondervan, 1987).
Carolyn Johnson, *Understanding Alcoholism* (Grand Rapids: Zondervan, 1991).
Chris Lutes, *What Teenagers Are Saying about Drugs and Alcohol* (Grand Rapids: Zondervan, 1987).

Daddy's Little Girl

At a convention, a beautiful blond girl came to talk to me, waiting until we were alone. For quite a few minutes, she couldn't stop crying. Finally she told me she was a Christian, but had been date-raped by her non-Christian boyfriend on one of their first dates. After the anger and humiliation had subsided, she found herself going back out with him. She was still involved with him in a regular, sexual relationship—though not without huge feelings of guilt.

On another retreat, a young girl confided that she had been date-raped at age thirteen. Humiliated, mortified, and ashamed, she proceeded to jump into relationships that always included sex because she felt "worthless." Now, at fifteen, she couldn't stop the pattern and had been sexually involved with at least sixteen guys.

Both of these girls' lives—and millions of others, I'm afraid—have been devastated and twisted into something they were never meant to be, all because they were forced to have sex while on a date.

Have no doubt about it: rape is not the victim's fault. If your date forces you into having sex—*even though he is your date*—he is at fault, and you can prosecute him for rape. If you are date-raped, *at least* tell someone who can help you deal with the trauma.

Many variables play a part in situations like these, but I'm finding more and more young women who are telling me they have been coerced into sex on dates. Girls, you need to take precautions. Do you mind if I give you some advice?

1. Early in your dating relationship, officially introduce your date to your parents. If you feel embarrassed or ashamed to do this (because of his age, looks, etc.), perhaps that feeling is giving you a clue that you might be in over your head. I'm not trying to make you paranoid or afraid to date, but I think you and your parents should know a person well before you agree to going out *alone* on a date.

2. Carefully select the clothes you wear on a date. Are they too low cut? Too short? Too tight? You might look smashing, but you might also look *too* tempting for your date's hormones to handle.

3. If you agree to secretive plans, such as going to a hotel party or to someone's house without chaperones, *you* may have lost your ability to stay in control of a certain situation.

4. Always carry extra money for a cab or phone call. This may seem unusual, but sometimes saying no could mean that you need to get your own ride home.

5. Finally, the only person you should even consider dating is a Christian—someone whom you *already know* has similar values, morals, and beliefs, and someone who *lives by those beliefs.*

Kim Boyce's song "Not for Me" makes a great point:

> He's not for me
> He doesn't know my Savior
> Not for me
> Had to let him go, oh, no
>
> He's not for me
> He would only want to change me

Not for me
Oh, no . . . no, oh, no.[1]

• • • • •
LIVE IT OUT!

Take a look at the following Scriptures and note how they *do* —or *should*—apply to your life:

2 Corinthians 6:14 _____

Ephesians 5:3–6 _____

1 Thessalonians 4:3–8 _____

2 Timothy 3:1–7 _____

Psalm 119:9 _____

Drawing the Line

It's inevitable. The day you start your diet, someone offers you a brownie or asks you to go out for ice cream! Why is it that you seem to get attacked at the very moment you set your mind on overcoming an enemy?

It may be food or cigarettes or swearing. Lots of students have confessed their desire to quit something but with *no* success!

I would like to do my best to motivate you *right now*— wherever you are in your battle. *No matter what problem you face, you cannot get through this without the ultimate defender, Jesus.* Why?

1. *He understands.* Hebrews 2:18 and 4:15 remind us that (a) he was tempted, yet never sinned, (b) he suffered when he was tempted, and (c) he sympathizes with us in our temptation.

2. *He has a way out for you.* In 1 Corinthians 10:13 Paul says, "No temptation has seized you except what is common to man. And God is faithful; he will not let you be tempted beyond what you can bear. But when you are tempted, he will also provide a way out so that you can stand up under it." This is an incredible Scripture to apply to your life *whenever* (I'm serious about this) you come to the end of your ability to fight off temptation. You can actually pray these words: "Lord, you said you won't force me to handle more than I can endure, so please provide an escape." Then trust him to be faithful to his promise, and be willing to take the escape route he provides!

You *must* call on him in your need. According to 2 Corinthians 10:5, we are to "take every thought captive" to Jesus. In my own life, and ever since my early days of abstaining from drugs, alcohol, and swearing, when a thought comes to mind that I know is not from God and will distract or even destroy me, I say to myself, "I rebuke that thought in the name of Jesus." Repeat it as many times as the thought comes back to you. Try it!

• • • • •
LIVE IT OUT!

I'm serious about your assignment today. I'd like you to *memorize* (put into your heart and mind) 1 Corinthians 10:13, and use this passage as a weapon when you are in a tempting situation.

Here's the verse again: "No temptation has seized you except what is common to man. And God is faithful; he will not let you be tempted beyond what you can bear. But when you are tempted, he will also provide a way out so that you can stand up under it."

LIVE IT! *with All Your Heart*

The Neon Lights of a Disciple

Fluorescent neon lights flash, blink, and blaze. They attract your attention. They force your eyes to notice them. They advertise something special. You just can't miss those neon lights.

How can you tell the neon lights of a Christian? This short Scripture study describes how true disciples act in order to shine with the light of Christ.

• They *Deny themselves for Christ* (Luke 9:23–25). They count the cost. They turn from who they were, and from what they wanted to be, in order to be whom the Lord wants them to be.

• They are *Involved in disciple making* (Matthew 28:16–20). They find ways to participate in spreading the good news of Christ in their homes, schools, neighborhoods, cities—in the whole world.

• They *Stick to Jesus' teachings* (John 8:31). Their goal is to handle the word of God accurately and to obey what they learn from it (2 Timothy 3:16; John 15).

• They *Carry their crosses daily and follow Jesus* (Luke 14:27). They are known as Christians (followers of Christ) to their families and friends.

• They *Invest in others' lives* in order to bear fruit for God's glory. They're willing and able to share their personal testimonies with others so as to lead them to salvation through Christ (John 15:8, 16).

• They *Put their faith in Christ* (John 2:11). They are growing to understand faith (Hebrews 11) and what it means to lead lives full of faith in the living God (Galatians 2:20).

• They *Love each other* (John 13:35). And people notice how they demonstrate that love.

• They give *Everything over to Christ* (Luke 14:33). They are willing to sacrifice dreams, possessions, and time to God. They've found that God doesn't just want a big part of their life—he wants it *all*!

• • • • •
LIVE IT OUT!

Ask yourself these questions, or share them with a friend:

D What has it cost you to be a disciple of Christ?

I What kind of short-term missions project would you be willing to consider going on?

S What is your daily time of Bible reading and prayer like? Describe.

C How well do your friends at school know you are a Christian? How about your family?

I Have you ever led someone to Christ or shared your testimony in public? Explain.

P How would you define faith?

L On a scale of 1 to 10, how would you rate your love for other Christians?

E Is there anything you are holding onto—or that is holding you back—from being an all-out disciple of Christ?

Led by the Spirit

Have you ever done something you didn't really want to do but kept feeling the need to do, only to find out afterwards that *God* wanted you to do it? That is one way, I believe, that the Holy Spirit works in our lives. When we are looking to God and listening, he often may direct our thoughts and actions toward something we hadn't planned on.

The other day I had to lug sixteen boxes to the post office, a chore I had been putting off because I was alone and couldn't figure out how I'd get the boxes out of the car and into the usual long line without making numerous trips.

Finally I loaded up the car and prayed, "Lord, I need help. If there's a parking space near the front door, I'll attempt this now. Otherwise, I'll wait 'til later when someone can help me."

As I pulled into the usually crowded post office, the parking spot closest to the door was empty. *Hmm, God has gone ahead of me*, I thought. But I hadn't yet checked to see how long the line inside was. I grabbed five boxes and stumbled through the door. Only three people in line! Immediately I moved into high gear, dropped the boxes behind the three people, and ran out to the car for another load.

On the car seat I saw a copy of my book, *Life of the Party*. Remembering that a postal clerk had asked me for a copy, I tossed it on top of my pile and hustled inside. No one else had gotten in line yet. Leaving behind a four-foot-high stack of boxes and my book on top for the clerk, I ran out for my last load. When I returned, gasping for air, I still had my place in line. Again I thought, *God really helped me out here.*

Then the guy in front of me turned and pointed to my book. "Where'd you get that?" he inquired.

"Oh, umm," I stammered, feeling kind of sheepish, "it's my book . . ." Before I could even finish, he said, "Where can I get one?"

"Oh, you can't yet," I said. "They won't be in bookstores for another month. Why? Are you a Christian?"

"No," he said shyly. "I'm an alcoholic, and I've been in treatment."

I was amazed. At that moment I believed God wanted him to have my story of being an alcoholic and finding healing and hope in Christ. So I said, "Here—take it!"

He seemed very grateful. And I couldn't help but think that God, by his Holy Spirit, had nudged and prodded me to take all those boxes to the post office on that particular day, just for the sake of that young man!

And if that wasn't enough, the man carried all my boxes to the counter for me!

● ● ● ● ●
LIVE IT OUT!

Plan a time to read the entire book of Galatians in one sitting—this week if possible. Pray first, asking God to show you something new and to give you powerful insight into what it means to live by the Spirit and to keep in step with him.

If the person of the Holy Spirit still seems confusing to you, use a concordance to read up on who he is and how you can't live without him. Look under "Holy Spirit" and read every reference!

A Gift for Me?

I was a one-hour-old Christian when Ralph, the person who led me to Christ, handed me a little book. He said it explained how God gives a gift—a special, God-given capability—to each believer in order for him or her to be an effective, functioning part of Christ's body on earth.

Well, how about that, I thought. *Here I am, a brand-spanking-*

new Christian and I already have something special to do for the Lord! Eagerly I nabbed his little book and headed home.

When I opened it later, however, I realized it was all new lingo to me. Prophecy, service, tongues, teaching? Each chapter listed various spiritual gifts and Scripture references like this:

Romans 12:6-8	Ephesians 4:7-13	1 Corinthians 12:1-11
prophecy	apostle	wisdom
service	prophet	knowledge
teaching	evangelist	faith
encouraging	pastor	healing
giving	teacher	miracles
leadership		prophecy
mercy		discernment
		tongues
		interpretation of tongues

As I studied the book, it didn't occur to me that a gift is selected and given by the giver—*not* by the recipient. So, like a nut, I prayed and asked God for every gift!

Before long, I became aware of one of my spiritual gifts—evangelism! I couldn't help but tell everyone about Jesus—salespeople, cashiers, postal workers, fellow employees, bosses, even all of my old buddies.

My new Christian friends also noticed that I had the gift of evangelism, so they laid hands on me and prayed that I might share Christ throughout the world. (So far, I've evangelized throughout the United States, Canada, and Japan—and it looks like I'm on my way to Singapore!)

Not long after I had pored over every page of my spiritual-gifts booklet, I attended a retreat where we studied—you guessed it—spiritual gifts. I even took a spiritual gifts test. I learned a lot about God, myself, others, and the church during that retreat. It confirmed what Ralph had hinted to me: God did have a plan for my life, and it was linked to my spiritual gift. What a trip!

Within a few months, I started working for Youth for Christ, a national Christian youth ministry, and have spent the last fourteen years in youth ministry! Hmm. It all fits. Quite interesting, and very exciting!

• • • • •
LIVE IT OUT!

What's your spiritual gift? If you're not sure, try the following:

1. Study the Scriptures listed above with your small-group leader, youth pastor, or friends.

2. Ask God, in prayer, to begin to reveal his gift to you.

3. Then look for confirmation
   • through his Word
   • from those in authority over you
   • from Christian friends
   • in Christian service and
   • through his Holy Spirit

4. Record your findings.

Faithfulness: A Lost Art?

Some words seem too serious to think about—words such as *faithfulness*. But when you really understand what a great quality it is to possess, *faithful* soon becomes a word you would like people to think about *you*! A faithful person is loyal, honest at all times, consistent and can be counted on. Do you know anyone like that?

Here's what it takes to be faithful as a student:

Be faithful with your parents. Be honest with them. Tell them the truth, even when it hurts. Don't leave out facts when detailing and promoting your social life. Spend their money wisely. Represent their name honorably. Honesty is the best policy.

Be faithful at school. Be truthful with your teachers. Don't cheat on papers, homework, and tests. Even if you fail, you'll have self-respect and (hopefully) the desire to do better next time. Don't con your teachers or ditch classes; little habits develop into big ones that are hard to break.

Be faithful to your friends. Be loyal. Don't two-time anyone. It's hard to live down a bad reputation. Remember, you reap what you sow. If you don't want to go out with your friends (or don't think it's wise), tell them the truth rather than make up a lame excuse. Don't put pressure on a friend to sin. Don't make your friends feel guilty or stupid by asking them to do something they're not comfortable doing.

Be faithful to God. Obey him. He really loves you. He needs your witness at school, in your home, with your friends. He's done a lot for you. Love him back (John 14:15).

• • • • •
LIVE IT OUT!

Take time today to think about *your* faithfulness record. With whom do you need to start over?

_____

Below, list the top two areas of your life that need a faithfulness brush-up.

1. _____

2. _____

Now list some practical ways you can acquire faithfulness in each of these areas (write a note of apology, renew an old friendship, etc.):

1. _____ 1. _____

2. _____ 2. _____

3. _____ 3. _____

4. _____ 4. _____

Now take a look at these Scriptures about faithfulness: Proverbs 3:3; Lamentations 3:22–23; Hebrews 10:23; Ephesians 4:15.

Is Your Heart after God?

My favorite book in the Bible is the book of Psalms. Lots of people think the Psalms are pretty boring—at first. I was a Christian a long time before I even read them!

But my mind really changed about the Psalms when I realized they were a lot like a prayer journal. They included poems, confessions, and praises to God by people such as King David. That's when I got hooked! I couldn't believe how open and honest David was with God about his feelings, fears, disappointments, promises, affections, and hopes. David sometimes confided in God as his best friend, at other times as a counselor, often as a Father— and always as Lord of his life. He hid nothing from God, and loved him with *all* of his heart. By looking in on David's prayer life, and by reading and praying the Psalms myself, I too am learning to grow a heart after God.

LIVE IT OUT!

It's apparent that some love God with all their heart, some with half a heart and some with not much heart at all. Is *your* heart after God? Why or why not?

Take the Psalms Challenge. Read one psalm a day until you finish the whole book (150 psalms). Keep a journal of your daily insights—and see if you begin to grow a heart after God! Start with Psalm 1 today!

A Battle in the Mind

A new school year had started. As a youth worker, I was always looking for volunteers to hang out with my students . . . *until* a skinnier, cuter, funnier, college-age volunteer wandered onto my turf.

Though I had often been overwhelmed with relationships as a Campus Life Director and cheerleading coach, I felt a wincing pain when "my" high school girls became friends with this particular volunteer. I should have called it jealousy from the start, but I didn't. I let the feelings grow. It became a battle in my mind.

Because I didn't want people to like her more than me, I schemed of ways to keep distance between her and the kids. I figured she never knew what I was feeling. And I kept trying to deny the feelings myself.

But my jealousy didn't just stay in my mind; it began to show itself in strange ways. I grew irritable and less friendly, even introverted at times (highly unusual for me!). I would get angry at other people if I thought they were encouraging her. I should have realized that my thoughts were causing me to sin, yet I even pushed *that* thought away.

But the thoughts simply wouldn't go away. They became more frequent, more intense, even destructive to my ministry. When they began consuming me, I finally realized that I had to talk to someone I could trust. I could barely initiate the discussion, because talking about my situation was very embarrassing (mostly humiliating) for me. But when I admitted to myself, to my counselor, and to God that jealousy was controlling me, I broke down and cried hard. I felt ashamed and terribly sorry that the situation had blown up to these proportions.

After getting it all out in the open, the gnawing feelings left, and they were replaced by the relief that comes with confession and forgiveness.

Next, I determined to tell her of the jealousy I'd been harboring toward her for the past six months. It would be hard, but I knew that admission would complete the confession and healing process I had read about in James 5:16.

But before I got the chance, she moved out of town.

Thinking about the situation after she left showed me what I had lost—a potential friend and ministry volunteer with whom I had a lot in common. We could have encouraged each other, been prayer partners, even close friends. Man, I had really blown it. Eventually I wrote her a long, humbling letter.

Through that experience I learned a tough lesson: When temptation knocks, don't let it in! Recognize it exactly for what it is. Identify it by its physical symptoms and its character-draining capabilities. Then get rid of it *quickly!* Don't dwell on it or think about it. Otherwise you may end up with a huge battle in your mind!

• • • • •

LIVE IT OUT!

What can you identify right now that has been knocking on the door of your mind, looking for a place to settle in? Check one, or write it in:

☐ Envy   ☐ Jealousy   ☐ Bitterness

☐ Sexual fantasies   ☐ Lust   ☐ Anger

☐ Other _____

Now what? Curb it. Stop it. Label it. Avoid it. Kick it out. Plot against it. Pray about it. Confess it as sin, and if necessary, admit it to someone else. Make it a practice to dwell only on good stuff (Philippians 4:8). Memorize Philippians 2:3–4 for future battles.

Come Follow Me

Author Tim Hansel coined a phrase with the title of his book, *Holy Sweat.* The phrase pretty accurately sums up the Christian life: *holy* is a high calling, and *sweat* is what it takes to get there!

It may not exactly sound exciting to you, but here's the deal: Whether you're in high school or on Wall Street, being a Christian is not just kicking back and enjoying yourself. It takes guts and courage and hard work. It means sacrifice. And giving. And giving again. It means change and discipline and endurance. It means growing and stretching. It demands turning from evil and loving what is pure and good. Sweat might mean working in missions, volunteering at your church, helping the poor, or tithing.

Yet God calls,
"Will you follow me?
Will you get to know me?
I need you."

• • • • •
LIVE IT OUT!

Take a look at these Scriptures: Philippians 2:13; 1:6; Ephesians 6:7–8; Colossians 3:23–24; Matthew 16:24. Then ask yourself, "Have I worked up a sweat lately?"

LIVE IT! Up!

From Knowing to Growing

Inches and centimeters measure height.

Pounds and kilograms measure weight.

Miles and kilometers measure distance.

But how do you measure *growth* in your relationship with God?

Once you've met Christ, you know him. But what does G-R-O-W-T-H in Christ look like?

Genuine love for God is increasing. You have actual feelings for him. You *want* to spend time with him. You find yourself telling others about him. This love for God should be getting stronger the longer you know him. (In fact, to develop that love, try writing a letter to God about how you feel toward him.)

Relationships are becoming more loving. You find it easier to forgive. Your temper doesn't flare up as much as before. You are more understanding. You look for what's right in a relationship, rather than what's wrong. You are becoming more gentle and kind; the fruits of the Holy Spirit (love, joy, peace, etc.—see Galatians 5:22) are showing more often.

Obedience is becoming a way of life. This area might be tougher for some than others. If, for example, your lifestyle was "wild and crazy" before you became a Christian, then your behavior should be growing more Christlike in very obvious ways to yourself and others. If, on the other hand, your life wasn't that wild before you became a Christian, your obedience to Christ would take the form of renewed thinking—changed attitudes, submission to authority, a willingness to confess sin in your life, and the growing ability to avoid what tempts you.

Worldly desires are decreasing. The things of the world—possessions, popularity, etc.—aren't as important as they once were in your life. You evaluate your priorities often and make adjustments according to God's Word. For instance, over the course of your high school years, your personal goals might change as your relationship with God grows. You may feel called to some kind of Christian service rather than to the business field. Your musical preferences may change. Who your friends are, what you read, how you dress—everything about you will reflect your desire to please God rather than the world.

Trust in God is deepening. You spend time in prayer and the Word—regularly! You constantly ask God for his advice when making decisions—and then you look and wait for his answers. You are learning to say to God, "I trust you, even when I don't understand your ways." Your faith in God is real. It affects all areas of your life: sports, school, family, friends, and is growing stronger daily.

Hunger for the Word of God is increasing. You are finding that the Bible is a source of guidance and hope for you, a place where you can hear God's voice. You look forward to reading it regularly and learning from it. You work at making your Bible studies and devotional life fresh and meaningful. You schedule your Bible reading times and memorize verses.

● ● ● ●
LIVE IT OUT!

Rate yourself from 1 to 10 (10 being highest) in these six areas of spiritual growth. Jot down today's date, and then turn back to this page in a month and see if you've grown in any of the areas.

	Today (Date: ____)	A Month Later (Date: ____)
Genuine love for God	_____	_____
Relationships are more loving	_____	_____
Obedience is a way of life	_____	_____
Worldly desires are decreasing	_____	_____
Trust in God is deepening	_____	_____
Hunger for the Word of God	_____	_____

Be the Best!

As a competitive person, I was always striving to be the best at something. In fact, much of my disillusionment with high school stemmed from the fierce competition for grades, friends, and positions on the swim team, cheerleading squad, and student council. Even in my family, I had a secret desire to be better than the others.

Yet I never seemed to reach the top. I always seemed to fall short of the best.

When I became a Christian, I discovered that I was in a new competition—a race—and this one offered a prize! In his New Testament letters, Paul mentions the race that Christians are to run. "Straining toward what is ahead," he wrote to the Christians in Philippi, "I press on toward the goal to win the prize for which God has called me heavenward in Christ Jesus" (Philippians 3:13–14).

"Do you not know that in a race all the runners run, but only one gets the prize?" he asked the Corinthians. "Run in such a way as to get the prize. . . . I do not run like a man running aimlessly; I do not fight like a man beating the air. No, I beat my body and make it my slave so that after I have preached to others, I myself will not be disqualified for the prize" (1 Corinthians 9:24, 26–27).

Athletics was a way of life I understood. That's why Paul's

insights into racing were incredibly motivating to me. I got excited to look at my Christianity as a race, especially one that I could win—prize and all! But my race wasn't *against* other runners, but more like a solo marathon—an *individual* course set before me.

It was up to me to train lazily or strenuously. But the prize was so worth winning that I wanted to do my *personal* best! I knew that reaching the goal would take hard work, discipline, saying no at times, maybe even changing some of my plans and habits. But I knew God's Word would give me the "course strategy" to reach the top—that is, to be the very *best* Christian that I could be!

• • • • •
LIVE IT OUT!

Draw a diagram of your race. Where is the starting point? What obstacles are in your immediate way? Any you can foresee down the road (maybe people or habits)? Where do you see the finish line?

List any obstacles: _____

_____

_____

Reach the T.O.P.

It's been said, "If you fail to plan, you've planned to fail." If you want to be successful, here are three strategies to help you to reach the T.O.P.:

Training strategy
Opposition strategy
Perseverance strategy

Training strategy: Training takes hard work, and it means *daily* discipline. I often think about the time and effort that Olympic athletes put into their training—the sacrifices they make, the social lives they give up in order to be their very best in competition. They have a goal. And so do Christians! Our training will make or break us. No pain, no gain. Decisions, determination, and disciplined lifestyles will develop strength, skills, and results that will draw us closer to our prize. But the lack of those very same things will keep us from reaching that goal.

So hang in there! Don't give up, even when you don't see immediate results. Press on. Be tough. Don't quit! Hard work *will* pay off in the end; your reward *will* come.

> No discipline seems pleasant at the time, but painful. Later on, however, it produces a harvest of righteousness and peace for those who have been trained by it. (Hebrews 12:11)

Opposition strategy: In this race you have no competition— but you do have an enemy! "You were running a good race," Paul wrote to the Christians in Galatia. "Who cut in on you and kept you from obeying the truth?" (Galatians 5:7). There are tons of obstacles in the way of teenage Christians who run their races—parties, drugs, sex, drinking, and cheating, to mention a few. *Look out*—for the enemy wants to trip you up. "The thief comes to steal, kill, and destroy," Jesus warned us in John 10:10. He's out there to ruin your faith and cause you to mess up your race. Be wise. You *need* to surround yourself with people who will point out the enemy's traps and help you to maneuver around them. Don't be naive— compromising will not keep you in the race! Recognize your enemy, watch for his schemes, know your weaknesses, and be on guard!

Perseverance strategy: Always remain confident. A positive attitude can strengthen your endurance during tough times, just as a negative attitude can sap your strength. It's not just in school, but in all of life that you will need to persevere. In Hebrews, the believers are really challenged to . . .

> not throw away your confidence; it will be richly rewarded. You need to persevere so that when you have done the will of God, you will receive what he has promised. (Hebrews 10:35– 36)

Therefore, since we are surrounded by such a great cloud of witnesses, let us throw off everything that hinders and the sin that so easily entangles, and let us run with perseverance the race marked out for us. Let us fix our eyes on Jesus. (Hebrews 12:1–2)

So stay in the race! Don't stop trying. Don't give up. There is a reward! Take off—throw off—the weights holding you back.

• • • • •

LIVE IT OUT!

The race has been marked out for you—so be your best! Develop a personal strategy for *Training*, for strengthening yourself against your *Opposition*, and for increasing your *Perseverance*:

Training: I need to train myself more diligently in (my words, my thoughts, my health, etc.) _____

_____

Opposition: I'm most easily tripped up by _____

_____

Perseverance: I need more confidence when it comes to _____

_____

I've got to get rid of these weights or hindrances (jealousy, wrong friends, a poor self-image, etc.) _____

_____

Would you pray a prayer like this?

Dear God, help me to run the race to which you've called me. Please, give me both the help and the hope to be the best I can be for the glory of your name.

Want to read more about this? Pick up a copy of *The Screwtape Letters*, by C. S. Lewis, or *This Present Darkness*, by Frank Peretti.

As the
World Turns

I read a Scripture yesterday that told me what Jesus thought of the world. "The world must learn," he told his friends and followers, "that I love the Father and that I do *exactly* what my Father has commanded me" (John 14:31).

Jesus had to deal with religious leaders who constantly bugged him, trying to convince him to attend dinner here, avoid those people over there, notice the wealthy, ignore the sick, do this and don't do that. Even his family and friends had their own set of expectations for him!

But Jesus set the record straight. He told them that the world had to learn something about him: that he loved his Father. In fact, his love was so great that he would do *whatever* his Father asked him rather than give in to all the expectations and pressures in the world.

Let's say you're sitting in school, and a buddy taps you on the shoulder and says, "Hey, let's ditch and go out for lunch." Or your boyfriend or girlfriend pressures you to go farther physically than you believe is right. A tug at your heart says, "I really shouldn't do this. In fact, I don't even *want* to do this." How do you say what you believe is right without feeling like a fool or losing their friendship? What can you do?

Remember what Jesus said. The world must learn that we love the Father, and that we are willing to do exactly what he has commanded us to do!

Whether you tell them flat out or write a note, whether you excuse yourself quietly or simply disappear, you've *got* to let them know that you love the Father and you want to do exactly what pleases him.

LIVE IT OUT!

Take a few minutes now to think about your world, the temptations you face, the people who pressure you. Ask God to show you any situation in which you need to let others know that you love the Father. How are you going to tell or show them? Do you need to do something today?

What Does God Want from Me?

I always fought with my mom when she asked me to clean my room. And wouldn't you know—now the tables have turned. Now *I'm* the mom, and my son has a habit of getting me to repeat myself ten times before doing what I ask!

It's almost a ritual between us. "Jake, would you make your bed?" Five minutes later: "Jake, would you please make your bed?" Another five minutes: I give him "the look" and slowly, threateningly say, "Jake—Make . . . your . . . bed!"

Then—and only then, it seems, he rushes into his room and makes his bed.

Things are changing, however. The other morning Jake walked into the family room and said, "Mom, I made my bed." I looked at him and thought, "What's wrong with him? What does he want now?" But Jake had gotten the picture. Because he loved me and knew I really wanted him to develop the habit of making his bed, he had decided to obey me. No big deal. No pushing. No nagging. No threats. He simply showed me that he loved me by obeying my desires—and we *both* felt good about it!

When you love someone, it becomes a whole lot easier to do things for them. You begin to enjoy making them happy! You want to show them how much they mean to you by doing what they ask of you!

John 14 talks a great deal about what God *wants* from us. Jesus explained it simply in verse 15: "If you love me, you'll obey me." He also gave the flip side: "He who doesn't love me won't obey me." Then later he added, "These words are not my own; they belong to the Father who sent me."

It all seems rather clear: If you love God, you'll obey him—and if you don't want to obey him, then perhaps you don't really love him.

Is loving God too much for him to ask of us?

• • • • •
LIVE IT OUT!

When you think about your relationship with God, in what particular area has he been asking you to obey? _____

_____

How can you show him you love him? _____

_____

Make time during the rest of this week to specifically show him your love by obeying him in this area. Pray and ask for his help, his forgiveness, and then for the ideas and motivation to succeed. Read and memorize Proverbs 16:3. Make it your prayer.

Have Yourself Committed

Getting married or becoming a parent is a huge commitment. But in order to *keep* such a commitment, people have to make decisions about it every day.

Being a committed Christian *should* mean giving one's total life to the Lord Jesus Christ. But I've noticed that in high school, students often hesitate in giving God all they've got because they might miss out on something, or because they might have to give up or change something in their lives.

Jesus said, "For whoever wants to save his life will lose it, but whoever loses his life for me will find it" (Matthew 16:25). It comes down to a decision—actually many decisions, most of them costly. A Christian must *daily* decide to follow God.

When students enter junior high or high school, they are different people than when they first made "commitments" to Christ at a younger age. So I often encourage students who decided as a young child to follow Christ to make the same decision or commitment as a young adult. In fact, even as an "old" adult myself, I like to pray the words of Psalm 37:5–6 and remind myself every morning, "I commit my ways to you, O Lord."

It's one thing to *believe* that Jesus died, rose again, and ascended into heaven, but it's hard to *live out* that belief in America today. With all the opportunities that can turn you away from the Lord, especially as a young person, a daily decision with your mind and heart to *live* as a believer will make a big difference!

• • • • •

LIVE IT OUT!

How's your Commitment Quotient? Do you live life saying one thing but doing another? Can you think of a recent situation where that happened? _____

_____

Start today with this prayer:

I have decided that I will live *this* day like a believer. Please, Lord. Help me. Show me today how I can live what I believe. Please direct my thoughts and my choices all through this day.

Perhaps you'd like to go one more step: *Write* your own prayer of commitment to God every day this week. Be specific in your commitment of time, your plans, and even your future. See if it makes a difference in your daily decisions. Consider making this simple, short prayer a lifetime habit.

The Time of Your Life Is Now!

Lisa asked Christ into her life as a freshman while on a Campus Life Breakaway trip. She was already popular, but because of her new life, her high-school years were filled with tough decisions about friendships, who to vacation with, which parties to attend or avoid, and who to date. She *constantly* struggled with making those decisions as a Christian. They never got easy for her.

But I noticed that she always had friends. Everyone really liked her, even though they knew her Christian beliefs and standards. In fact, she was an active member of the Campus Life club at school, attended a weekly Bible study, and often invited her closest friends to come along.

In her senior year, Lisa was the only girl selected to the Homecoming Court who wasn't a cheerleader, majorette, or band member. I couldn't help but think of all the times she had worried and wondered: "Has my faith really made a difference? Has anyone even noticed? Or have all those struggles and tough decisions been for nothing?"

That balmy Friday night, her questions were answered. At the halftime coronation ceremony, Lisa's name boomed out over the loudspeaker as Homecoming Queen!

At last she knew she had gained the respect of the people in her high school. Being a Christian had *not* kept her from having the time of her life. In fact, Lisa found that her faith in Christ had *made* those years into the time of her life!

Most high schoolers I've met approach God in one of two ways:

1. "I'll wait 'til I'm older before I make Christ the center of my life." Or,

2. "I can't live *without* Christ being the center of my life."

Those who recognize their need for Christ while in high school will often get involved in a campus Christian organization or a youth group at church as their source of social life and spiritual support. They may or may not be invited to parties, or asked to hang out with the most popular group, but they don't have a lot of regrets about it either. And because they aren't living a double life, they can freely share their faith with their school friends, even invite them to Christian events. They are proud to be Christians.

● ● ● ● ●
LIVE IT OUT!

Turn to Ephesians 4 in your Bible. With a highlighter, pen, or pencil in hand, read the entire chapter and underline the verses that challenge you or encourage you right now in your life with Christ. When you are finished, ask God to give you his strength and his Holy Spirit to help you live your life *now* for him. Don't be afraid to let go of anything that could be holding you back. Say with Paul, "I am not ashamed of the gospel, because it is the power of God for the salvation of everyone who believes" (Romans 1:16).

Dear *Live It!* Reader:

I hope this daily devotional has encouraged you in your
relationship with God . . . because that's the bottom line!
How much we feel love and loyalty toward God as our
Friend, Lord, and Savior will determine how we will live for
him. My true prayer is that this book will cause you to know
God better and to make him known!

If you are interested in getting in touch with me or in
ordering my *Quietimes Student Prayer Notebook* (or any of
my other tapes or books), please write to me or call:

My Partner Ministries
Box 8862
Orange, CA 92664
714-633-7763